LED BY THE SPIRIT

LED BY THE SPIRIT

The Story of New York Theological Seminary

GEORGE W. WEBBER

The Pilgrim Press
New York

Copyright © 1990 by The Pilgrim Press
All rights reserved

No part of this publication may be reproduced, stored in a retrieval system, or transmitted in any form or by any means, electronic, mechanical, photocopying, recording, or otherwise (brief quotations used in magazines or newspaper reviews excepted) without prior permission of the publisher.

Scripture quotations are from the Revised Standard Version of the Bible, copyright 1946, 1952 and © 1971 and 1973 by the Division of Christian Education of the National Council of the Churches of Christ in the United States of America and are used by permission.

Library of Congress Cataloging-in-Publication Data

Webber, George W.
Led by the Spirit : the story of New York Theological Seminary / George W. Webber.
p. cm.
Includes bibliographical references.
ISBN 0-8298-0850-7
1. New York Theological Seminary. I. Title.
BV4070.N4653W42 1990
207′.7471—dc20 90-33340
CIP

The Pilgrim Press, 475 Riverside Drive, New York, NY 10115

CONTENTS

FOREWORD

In the fall of 1979, the newly employed development officer for New York Theological Seminary (NYTS) was at a training session in Indianapolis sponsored by the Lilly Endowment. During the course of one of the lectures the speaker warned the trainees that they should be careful in writing publicity articles about their seminaries. He suggested that they should, for example, never use a word like unique since all seminaries are more or less similar. They could talk about the distinctive features of their own institution, but it would be inappropriate to suggest that they were one of a kind. A Lilly Endowment staff member sitting next to the development officer from New York Theological Seminary leaned over and whispered, "This doesn't apply to you. New York Theological Seminary can certainly call itself unique."

This was not meant to suggest any special virtue or merit but underline the fact that beginning in 1970 New York Theological Seminary had dismantled the traditional patterns of a theological seminary and undertaken tasks quite different from those normally in the portfolio of institutions of theological education. There was neither any great new vision nor any special wisdom in the process but rather a crisis that had forced the seminary to discover a new sense of its vocation. This had resulted in its undertaking a variety of tasks that are not customary for graduate theological seminaries.

Nine difficult years had moved the institution to the verge of bankruptcy and had led to a general state of uncertainty. Located as it was in the heart of New York City, NYTS would seem to have a particular role in equipping men and women for urban ministry but an eight-year attempt in this direction from 1960 to 1968 had resulted in the termination of a president and an increased level of frustration.

Thus it was that in the spring of 1969, George W. (Bill) Webber was hired as the Chief Executive Officer in one last dire effort to find justification for continuing the institution. Bill Webber likes to report that during that first year he could go to work with a great sense of freedom in the confidence that nothing he could do could possibly make things worse. It was that ethos which enabled the trustees and faculty to embark on a year of theological experimentation no seminary short of such desperation would have been willing to undertake. It is precisely that freedom to experiment coupled eventually with the resources to undertake a range of new programs that explains the writing of this book. The uniqueness of New York Theological Seminary with its opportunity to undertake new tasks and experiment in untried paths, presents itself as a story that might well be shared with those concerned about higher education in general and theological education in particular. The purpose here is first to share the story of that early drama and subsequent history of the institution from 1968 to 1983 and second to examine in somewhat more detail the basic elements of the seminary's program as a way of sharing this experience with the world of theological education.

Much of what was to develop during these fifteen years grew out of the previous experiences of Bill Webber in urban ministry and in theological education, the reality of church life in New York City with its predominance of black and Hispanic churches, and the earlier traditions of the Biblical Seminary in New York, which in 1965 was renamed the New York Theological Seminary.

In addition to the story of these years from 1968–1983, a series of monographs (see Appendix D) have been prepared, discussing in much greater detail the key elements in the life and program of the seminary.

This study was undertaken at the request of the Lilly Endowment, Inc., which provided the necessary funds. It was determined that it should be written by Bill Webber. After some effort to write an objective history, he came to the conclusion that the task could best be served by undertaking the story in the first person, writing clearly from his own perspective. The trustees and faculty of New York Theological Seminary hope this study will stimulate the imaginations of educators and church leaders to discover new challenges and seek appropriate patterns of response.

Fr. WILLIAM R. NAUGHTON,
Chairman, Board of Trustees

INTRODUCTION

The Preparation of the President

I graduated from Harvard College in 1942 and along with my classmates had a choice of the army, navy, or air corps. I spent the next three and a half years in the navy mainly as a gunnery officer on a destroyer escort. Uncertain where I was headed during my college years, but feeling inclined to law school, I had, due to the war, suspended making any decision. Ordered after V. E. Day in June, 1945, to a ship in the Pacific, I stopped in Cambridge and bought three first-year law texts. Then, in August, the war was over and the necessity of a vocational decision could no longer be postponed. The law books were not exciting, but more importantly, there was a nagging feeling that perhaps I ought to consider the ministry. During those long hours on watch, with nothing really to do but reflect on what I could do with the rest of my life, I kept remembering that several persons of faith who had been strong influences as I was growing up seemed to have a sense of purpose, meaning, and joy in their work that was compelling. From Pearl Harbor in the fall of 1945, I wrote my wife that I thought I ought to give seminary a try. Surprised and incredulous, Helen agreed to the decision. This took us, in January, 1946, to Union Theological Seminary in New York City, hoping we could survive life in the heart of such a big city for the three years seminary would require.

Much of my senior year was spent studying the community of East Harlem at the behest of a seminary classmate, Don Benedict. Benedict was the only one of the eight Union Seminary students who, after serving prison terms for refusing to register for the draft in 1940, had returned to Union to complete his degree. It was his firm conviction that the gospel that he was studying at Union and preparing to proclaim, was truly for all people. The fact that inner-city ministry was virtually ignored by the denominations represented by Union students bothered him deeply. He was determined to begin his ministry among those whom the churches seemed to be ignoring, particularly at a time when home missions efforts were almost exclusively focused on creating new churches in the suburbs mushrooming all over the United States. As a result of our investigations in East Harlem, where we found no vital ministry on the part of any of the mainline denominations, we drafted a proposal for a new attempt at Protestant ministry in the inner-city. This became the East Harlem Protestant Parish (EHPP). There was not enough money for more than one of us to work full-time in East Harlem. To my relief, I found a good compromise through a position as veterans' advisor and later Dean of Students at Union Theological Seminary. This enabled me to work part-time and summers in East Harlem.

Union Seminary had a long history of relationships with this Upper East Side immigrant community, beginning with the founding of Union Settlement in 1895 by lay persons connected with the seminary. Many Union students had undertaken field work in the social agencies and churches of the neighborhood. Part of my work at the seminary quickly developed into supervising our students who worked in the East Harlem Protestant Parish. Thus emerged a persistent question in my ministry: how does one equip men and women for urban ministry, and what role can the seminary play in that undertaking?

The compromise of enjoying the life at Union, with the challenging role of dean of students and teacher, while working also in East Harlem as a member of the Group Ministry gradually became untenable. We felt as a family, that we had either to move to East Harlem and undertake our basic ministry there or cut our ties with the parish. With great trepidation we moved in April, 1957, to a low income public housing project in East

Harlem. That community has been our home to this day. Although I continued to teach at Union until 1973, I had clearly changed my base to the inner city.

The East Harlem Protestant Parish emerged at a time in the life of the Protestant churches when major energy was being given to building new suburban churches. It was assumed too readily by mission boards that communities like East Harlem, whether black, Hispanic or European immigrant, were either Roman Catholic or adequately served by other denominations. The parish discovered that in a community of approximately 215,000 people occupying only about one square mile, not more than ten percent of the population had any church connection. Thus the churches of the EHPP became in a very real sense a laboratory for exploring the role of historic denominations in this missionary world. Two factors were unique. The parish was supported by eight denominations, thus providing the occasion for all kinds of experiments and new patterns, since no one denomination could insist on its traditional operating style. At the same time, the staff was able to mobilize substantial funding from suburban churches, foundations, and individuals, which enabled them to exploit their freedom, to try a variety of approaches, and even to fail on many occasions.

The years from the beginning of the parish in 1948 through 1966 marked the period during which the World Council of Churches engaged in a series of studies on the role of the church in an urban, industrial world from which emerged a host of studies on the nature of the church and its mission. A number of themes sounded loud and clear. "The church exists for mission as a fire exists for burning" was an often quoted phrase from Emil Brunner. The Department of the Laity brought forcibly to our attention the nature of lay ministry. The studies in evangelism offered the notion of the church gathered for worship and dispersed for ministry. From the study secretary, Hans Hoekendijk, came the definition of evangelism as involving *kerygma*, *koinonia*, and *diakonia*. Amid all this ferment that falls under the category of "church renewal" was a strong emphasis on the centrality of Bible study and the recovery of biblical literacy by all who called themselves Christians.

The East Harlem Protestant Parish read and sometimes shared in the development of these studies. They often informed our efforts or provided clues that we explored in our work. Frequently we were visited by such of our theological mentors as D. T. Niles, Hans Hoekendijk, George MacLeod, Ted Wickman, Suzanne de Dietrich, and Horst Symanowski. The effects were seen in the strong emphasis in the parish on lay Bible study and biblical preaching, on the development of lay leadership, on our commitment to public ministry and mission, and in the commitment to a group ministry style with mutual accountability and discipline, including spouses and lay staff as well as clergy.

As the parish in its original form drew to a close and devolved into separate units of ministry about 1966, a major new development was being undertaken in New York City called Metropolitan Urban Service Training (MUST) with funding primarily from the United Methodist Church but with a genuinely ecumenical board. I was asked to organize this program and found myself involved in continuing education, a field in which I had very little experience or wisdom. The significance of MUST was its ability to provide funds for the staff, including myself, to work at developing the skills required in continuing education and to get a better understanding of what the church in an urban context should be about. It was great preparation for what was to come at New York Theological Seminary. It is also relevant to note that MUST rented its facilities from New York Theological Seminary, first in a building next door with use of classroom space and then on the whole tenth floor of the seminary's building.

The impetus for MUST grew out of the awareness that mainline churches, for all the interest in urban ministry during the ten-year period after 1955, had not made much of an impact. This sense of frustration had led to the development in Chicago of the Urban Training Center, an interdenominational program with quite extensive funding by the supporting churches and several foundations.[1] But from the perspective of the United Methodist Board of Missions, that approach was not adequately concerned with equipping individual con-

1. Cf. George Younger, *From New Creation to Urban Crisis 1987: A Study of the Urban Training Movement.*

gregations, clergy and laity for a vital urban presence, but rather was training for public ministry and new forms of presence. MUST was to focus quite specifically on education for clergy and laity, in the New York area, thus making possible genuine on-the-job training.

Out of this background of twenty years in urban ministry in New York City—Union Seminary, East Harlem, and MUST—there are three further experiences that were part of my preparation for New York Theological Seminary. First was the development of the Metropolitan Intern Program beginning in 1964 under my function as a Union professor and continuing under MUST. As part of my job description I had been asked specifically to find ways of relating Union's programs to the life of the city, and this had led to the development of a program for students in the year between college and seminary. This came during the period of growing concern and unrest over Vietnam when a great many students were enrolling in seminaries as much to discover their own personhood and values as to undertake specific preparation for ordained ministry, or perhaps simply to avoid the draft. The trial year program funded by Rockefeller money had encouraged students to undertake this exploration while attending a theological seminary. An alternative occurred to us. Why not provide a year for those planning to begin seminary that would combine a secular work experience with an intensive seminar devoted to exploring their own faith, life commitments, and vocational direction. This would be an interruption in the long years of academic routine, providing what Eric Erikson calls a "moratorium" in which to seek self-understanding and vocational clarity. Thus in the fall of 1964 a group of twelve students who had been admitted to seminary but had not yet begun full-time study moved into East Harlem, found jobs in a variety of social welfare and business programs in the city, and began a very intensive year of involvement and reflection. A description of the program sent out to prospective students read in part as follows:

Broad Objectives

A. Personal involvement in the life of the metropolitan society, with the opportunity for reflection on its nature and meaning. This provides a break from academic preparation and exposure to some of the crucial problems of the secular world.

B. Corporate and personal consideration of the "style of life" that is required for Christian presence and witness in the metropolis. Here the concern underlying our work is how students preparing for the ministry may discover and forge patterns of discipline, fellowship, and study that such a vocation requires.

C. Underlying the nature and task of the church in modern society. The interns will reflect theologically on the response the church is to make to the needs dramatically exposed in the metropolis.

The elements of the program included secular employment in the city, involvement in the inner-city community, where they were required to live, participation in the life of an urban congregation, and regular participation in ten hours of seminar meetings and study as a focus for reflection on their experiences, on their future direction, and on their faith development. The important clue that resulted from this metropolitan intern program was the fact that in all dealings with clergy, whether as seminary students or as ordained ministers, it is imperative to continue to work at the question of personal maturity. As Ephesians 4 suggests, the Christian is called to grow to the fullness of the stature of Christ, to mature personhood, a task that is never completed but to which attention must continually be given throughout one's life. Thus it has been that at New York Theological Seminary in all of our programs the question of authentic personhood has been a key factor. Laity seem desperately eager to have clergy with a clear sense of their own identity who are able to relate to them as authentic human beings.[2]

A second important insight that had emerged during the years of MUST was the importance of taking with very great seriousness the mandate of the seminary to function as a profes-

2. Cf. John Fletcher, *Religious Authenticity and the Clergy* (Washington D.C.: The Alban Institute, 1975).

sional school. So much of theological education has been highly academic, the practical disciplines taking secondary place in the curriculum or least in the sense of their importance in the minds of most faculty and students. About the time the MUST program was beginning, the first major conference to consider the role of continuing education in theological education was held at Andover Newton Theological School. I was present along with a number of seminary faculty, denominational executives, and a few parish clergy. One evening after the meeting, Scott Paradise (then with Detroit Industrial Mission), Reuel Howe (from the Institute of Advanced Pastoral Studies), and I went out for a talk. To our surprise, Howe gave us a very hard time, saying something to the effect, "I'm really frustrated by you young turks who are so cynical about the life of the church and who talk too dramatically about the need for new forms of missionary presence. You've got no business to be as harsh in your critique of the patterns of the church until you address one significant problem. From my point of view," he said, "the clergy have simply not been trained in the skills and competency required for effective ministry. And until we have competent clergy, you have no business making these judgments about the life of the church. Who knows what might be possible were the leaders of congregations able teachers, community analysts equipped with other skills that the kind of missionary church you seek requires?"

I remember being much taken aback by this challenge and took to heart Howe's admonition. Very clearly the focus of the MUST program was to examine the fundamental tasks that would be required for competent ministry in an urban congregation and to seek to equip clergy for these specific tasks. Howe himself was also convinced that this work of specific professional training could be done better outside the specifically academic context of the seminary and perhaps could be effectively developed in some pattern of on-the-job training immediately after the completion of the formal seminary degree. In this perspective the importance of urban training programs like MUST and the Institute for Advanced Pastoral Studies, which he had founded in Michigan was apparent.

Finally I was much influenced by a project of the Association of Theological Schools (ATS). This organization of accredited seminaries had grown in maturity and resources; it had undertaken a "futures" study that required a broad look at the state and future of the enterprise of theological education. The ferment in all higher education during the late sixties had reached into the life of the major nondenominational seminaries like Union and Yale with an impact in terms of student unrest that found both faculty and trustees ill-equipped to handle effectively. Societal issues growing out of the civil rights struggle, the beginnings of feminism, and especially the Vietnam War thrust themselves into the seminary communities. I remember vividly a young woman in my class at Union about 1970, telling me that she had been assigned by the women's caucus to monitor my sexist language.

In 1966 the executive director called together a group of eight seminary faculty and gave them an exciting task. Would they please let their imaginations run freely and develop what from their perspective would be ideal curriculum for theological seminaries in the 1970s. He told the group that they needn't give any consideration to whether any imaginable seminary faculty would be willing to implement such a curriculum, nor were they to worry about what it would cost. Rather he urged them to give free reign to their imagination—their best thought as what would be an ideal, exciting, and relevant seminary curriculum at the master of divinity level. That was a very stimulating challenge to the group (eight white males—reflecting the reality of theological education then and even today).

Very hard work over a number of months and several lengthy meetings resulted in what was published as the summer of 1968 issue of *Theological Education*, "The Curriculum for the Seventies." It clearly took into account concern for how students might grow in their personal maturity and faith and considered how more careful attention could be given to the particular skills required by the tasks of ordained ministry. But it also came down very strongly on the importance of how the basic academic disciplines of the seminary would be taught: what has become a cliché, the concept of "doing theology." The discussions focused on the need to teach theological disciplines in an interface with the context in which the church finds itself. They called this model "action/reflection," always seeking to relate theology and practice, faith and life, in the patterns of the curriculum. This way of "doing theology," which has since been strongly underlined by what liberation theology refers to as "praxis," was also supported by the development of the case method of teaching in theological education which had been undertaken by the Association of Theological Schools in cooperation with the Harvard Business School under a major grant from the Lilly Endowment.

For me, this "Curriculum for the Seventies" became a fascinating model of what a seminary might be. Thus it was with a considerable sense of anticipation that I came to realize that, in its desperation, New York Theological Seminary might be in position not just to see the curriculum as a distant challenge that might suggest a few clues as to how a seminary might move but to offer an honest possibility of trying to put its major elements into practice. It seemed that none of the other members of the group of eight could anticipate any serious opportunity to implement many of the suggestions, but suddenly for me this curriculum had the potential of becoming a reality.

The Background of New York Theological Seminary

The Auburn History of Theological Education in the United States makes it clear that the founding and early years of the Biblical Seminary marked the only enduring variant to the four-fold curricular pattern that had become normative with the founding of Andover Seminary. Wilbert Webster White, graduate of Wooster College, with a doctorate in biblical studies from Yale University, had taught in several seminaries and become troubled by what he saw as their failure to give proper attention to biblical studies. As he saw it, men were graduating from seminary, able to discourse on the issues of higher criticism, but were biblically illiterate. At the same time, graduates of conservative seminaries were prepared to fight for the inerrancy of scripture, but they too were often not familiar with large parts of the Bible. In 1900 White determined to found a seminary that would place the Bible at the center of the curriculum, not as one of four major elements, and to see to it that his graduates knew the scriptures from beginning to end. His inductive method of Bible study, which evolved while he was studying with William Rainey Harper, was designed to achieve this objective. From the testimony of many alumni, they did graduate with firm biblical knowledge and a method they found useful in missionary work all over the world.[3]

The seminary was located in the heart of Manhattan, had a significant number of women students and faculty from the beginning, and was thoroughly nondenominational and lay controlled. By charter, sixty percent of the trustees had to be laity and no more than seven could come from any one denominational tradition. These were all rare features. In addition, however, Dr. White did not believe in establishing an endowment. Without either denominational funding or the support of a college or university, this was a recipe for the serious financial troubles that began at the time of the Great Depression. This was compounded by the continued presidency of the founder at a time when his capacities were dimmed by age. Survival was barely managed during this period to the close of World War II, largely through cutting faculty salaries drastically, to the point of serious exploitation, use of bequests for current funding, and loyal alumni support.

The traditions of Biblical Seminary were maintained by Dean McKee, an able president, during the years from 1950–60. But he was in a continual battle for funds, for students, and for competent faculty. When he departed in 1960 for a teaching position elsewhere, the trustees determined that the time had come for a radical break with the past if the seminary was to survive. Their decision was to create a seminary designed to equip men and women for urban ministry, using the New York City location as a strong drawing card. Not long after, to avoid the image of a "Bible School" the name was changed to New York Theological Seminary.

But the attempt did not succeed. Within four years, the entire community—faculty, students and trustees—had come to

---

3. The "inductive method" included much of what is now being called "literary analysis."

the conclusion that the president, hired to build the new future, had to go. A successor was found who lasted less than two years, after developing severe ulcers. Only a small group of determined trustees were committed to the survival of the institution.[4]

The Social Situation in 1968

New York Theological Seminary, its students and faculty, did not seem to have been very much caught up in the ferment of the sixties. But the urban world all around had a decisive impact on the years that were to follow. For the future of the seminary, these factors are noteworthy. First was the civil rights movement that began with the Supreme Court decision in Brown v the Board of Education (1954) and continued with the emergence of Martin Luther King Jr. during the struggles in Montgomery, Alabama. Perhaps for the first time, it became apparent that racism was not simply a southern issue but a pervasive reality in all of American life. Now we had to face the fact that Harlem was indeed a ghetto, that racism in New York was in many ways more painful and destructive than in the south, where it was open and blatant, rather than hidden and indirect. There was hope that, once exposed, the problems of racism and discrimination would be faced and democracy would reach a new level of integrity. By 1968 these dreams were shattered by the murder of Dr. King and the manifest intransigence of racism. But the struggle was to continue with the commitment of a new generation of leadership. Perhaps most important was the legacy of self-confidence in the community. Now there was a clear awareness of the issues and above all a conviction that black was beautiful, that the future did not lie in the hands of white liberals but in the commitment of men and women to continue the struggle for justice.

With the civil rights movement had come the war on poverty, President Johnson's determination to face up to the issues so forcefully documented by Michael Harrington in *The Other*

---

4. For the history of the seminary prior to 1968, see Virginia Brereton, *The History of Biblical Seminary: 1900–1965*. Monograph VIII.

America. In East Harlem there had been a tremendous burst of hope as the rhetoric of the Great Society echoed through the streets. The urban riots in the sixties were, however, only one manifestation of the disillusionment that came with the painful discovery that like racism, poverty was not going to be easily overcome. In the early days of the work in East Harlem, apathy had been a powerful reality. Inner city men and women, without hope, blamed by society for their own situation, and thus truly victims, had then been awakened to a new hope that race and poverty were going to be attacked, that America would make good on its promises of equality and opportunity. When those hopes were smashed it was almost as though a form of psychic murder were being committed.

A third reality in the sixties was, of course, the undeclared war in Vietnam that had such a powerful impact on all of American life. It symbolized how once again our foreign policy was significantly determined by anticommunism and the conviction that the United States of America had to police the world. The war became a nightmare for President Johnson, the source of anguish for a whole generation of young men called to fight a war they did not understand in a world where they were total strangers against an enemy they hardly even saw. It spelled the end of any serious war on poverty and left a society badly shattered and confused.

Also of emerging significance was the feminist movement that, for me at least, had come to strong consciousness when I read *The Feminine Mystique* (1964). The impact of the increased awareness of sexism was to be felt in the ecclesiastical world. Biblical scholarship brought a sharp awareness of the sexism of biblical writers, translators, and particularly interpreters, thus helping many liberated women discover they could affirm a Christian faith with integrity. Harvard Divinity School admitted its first women students for the bachelor of divinity degree in 1954. Although the Congregational Churches had ordained women since 1853 and the United Methodist Church had permitted women into full standing for some years, opportunities were limited. It was 1957 before the United Presbyterian Church (U.S.A.) ordained its first woman and a decade later before the Episcopal Church was to act, and then only after a dramatic unorthodox ordination in Philadelphia. But by the mid-seventies, able women were filling nearly half the places in the (now) master of divinity (MDiv) programs of the leading university-based and nondenominational seminaries.

In a metropolitan area like New York City each of these four realities had a tremendous impact. Here racism had been revealed as a massive force. Here were the stark contrasts between rich and poor, often existing literally side by side. New York Theological Seminary, located in the heart of Manhattan, could no longer ignore these realities. It was to become truly the "New York Theological Seminary" or die.

This was also a time when these and other forces were creating something like a crisis in the life of churches in the United States. A severe malaise was infecting the ranks of clergy, Protestant and Catholic alike. The stream of ordained clergy leaving the ministry was increasing in volume each year, while their frustration was matched by those who remained in parish positions but at the price of a deep sense of alienation and discouragement. The customary pattern was to attribute this sad state of affairs to the rigidity or irrelevance of present ecclesiastical structures, the superficial commitment of many churches' members, and the present state of confusion in the churches over the mission and ministry. I had come to the conclusion, however, that in some significant degree the clergy were not equipped personally and professionally for faithful and effective ministry in the contemporary world. Often they held to an understanding of the nature and purpose of the church that grew up in small town or rural America, a world that no longer really existed. Sometimes they applied old models to situations where these are largely irrelevant. Other times they lacked either the personal maturity or skills required to give shape to an appropriate expression of their function. Perhaps at New York Theological Seminary I would have the opportunity to test these hunches and to think through a program of education for clergy and laity that would recognize the new situation in which the church found itself.

CHAPTER 1

The End of the Old, the Failure of the New

A Time for Radical Surgery 1968–1970

The situation at the beginning of the academic year 1968–69 was bleak. The seminary possessed a functional twelve-story building in the heart of the city on 49th Street between Second and Third Avenues in the posh Turtle Bay section of Manhattan, halfway between the Waldorf Astoria and the United Nations. The four-and-a-half floors of dormitory space, however, were only partially filled with students. Some space was rented out to a collection of women and men who worked in the midtown section of New York and a few retired persons with some modest connection with the religious community. But that still left a good deal of unrented space. The administration was in the hands of John Sutherland Bonnell who had retired some years before from a long pastorate at the prestigious Fifth Avenue Presbyterian Church. In retirement he had become a member of the board of trustees at the Seminary. When the previous president had resigned with a bad case of ulcers after less than two years in office, Bonnell had consented to serve as president for a brief interim until a successor could be found. He had now been at the helm for two years and had made clear his firm intention to leave no later than December 31, 1968. As had been his pattern during those years, he gave about half time to the position as president, leaving academic matters in the hands of Dean Kendig Cully and the business details to the comptroller, Paul Jensen.

The enrollment picture followed the pattern of the previous several years with less than 100 full-time equivalent students taking basic seminary work in religious education, bachelor of divinity (BD), or the master of sacred theology (STM) degrees. The one innovation that Bonnell had been able to bring about was the initiation of an STM degree in pastoral counseling, utilizing, for two-thirds of the requirement, the resources of the Post-Graduate Center for Mental Health located on 29th Street. This was the largest training center for mental health professionals in the country. The directors had been glad to help design a program to enhance the skills of parish clergy in their pastoral counseling. On the seminary side, the program was directed by a Lutheran clergyman, John Kildahl, who was a first-rate clinical psychologist with a large private practice in New York City. He took administrative responsibility for the program and taught several courses each semester while maintaining his practice.

As the year began, the overwhelming issue continued to be financial. The trustees had approved a budget with an anticipated deficit of well over $100,000, aware that if fund-raising efforts were not unusually successful, they would use all the remaining liquid assets of the seminary and presumably need to sell at least some of the property on 49th Street. The one positive factor was the strong determination of a small group of dedicated trustees who were convinced they could find a way to continue a seminary which, from their perspective, had made a great contribution over nearly seventy years. For them the urgent matter was to secure a new president.

Although underway for over a year, the presidential search process had so far been unsuccessful. One candidate who had been highly recommended took one look at the realities of the seminary and declined to be considered further. By the early fall the committee had been unable to find any agreement on other potential candidates. It was at this point that several members of the faculty advisory committee suggested they talk to me. Happily involved in a dual ministry combining a tenured position at Union Seminary and my work at MUST, I was in no mood to consider any possible role at a seminary whose future seemed so unpromising. Given the fact that there was in the city a wide range of seminaries, both liberal and evangelical, there seemed no obvious reason why New York Theological Seminary should continue the struggle and in the process presumably eat up all of its remaining assets. I had, however, no basis for refusing to talk with the chairperson of the trustees and then to meet informally in early November with the search committee. I very well remember my initial meeting late one afternoon with a small group of the trustees. On the one hand I tried to be polite, but on the other, I honestly had no interest in undertaking what seemed from a distance to be an impossible task. I remember smoking my pipe, asking very difficult questions, and making it quite clear that I was not a candidate for the job. Apparently this fact alone proved to be somewhat winsome and did not deter them from exploring my credentials further and then presenting my name to the trustees at a special meeting on December 17.

That evening I had a call from the chairman of the board, Harold Midtbo, who had been a deeply committed member of the trustees for some years and whose energy had been to a large degree responsible for the seminary's survival to this date. He informed me that I had been elected president and hoped very much I would accept this call. Having read the bylaws, however, I had a pretty good hunch that the legal requirements for electing a president had not been met, since it required an affirmative vote of a majority of the living trustees. I asked Mr. Midtbo what the vote had been and discovered it was six in favor, two against, and one abstention. Further questioning produced the fact that there were twenty-three trustees. I informed Mr. Midtbo that, since clearly there had not been a legal election, there really was no basis for proceeding. He urged me, however, to meet with him for further conversation. By this time my concern for the seminary had been increased a bit as I sensed the anguish of both faculty and students about what the future might be. In our conversation I agreed with Midtbo that, if the seminary wished, I would take some time over the course of the next six weeks to serve as a consultant to the trustees, examining the possibilities for the future, and trying to make sure we had surfaced the hard questions that had to be asked before they could with a sense of responsibility call anyone to be the president. A regular meeting of the trustees was due to be held in February, and we agreed that this would be the time for such a report. I made it quite clear that no call had been issued and that there was no responsibility on either side to assume that we were even involved in a serious courtship.

As a result of this agreement, I produced a report on February 3, 1969, called "The Future of The New York Theological Seminary." (See Appendix A.) I addressed it to the faculty as well as the trustees. Over the seminary's history, the faculty, who had the most invested in the institution, had rarely been consulted on any matter by the board of trustees, and thus they gave my memo serious attention. A copy also went to the student body suggesting that they respond to its content in a letter to the trustees. In reading the report in retrospect, I am a little shocked to discover that I had apparently by that time been convinced that there was the possibility of a future for the seminary and was willing to make myself available if the hard questions in the analysis could be answered. Eight months earlier, Randy Nugent and I had switched assignments at MUST. He took over as the director and I had become responsible for academic programs. This was an important way of signaling the constituency of MUST that it was now led by an able black leader with a white associate. The staff of MUST encouraged me to consider taking on the seminary with the hope that in its desperate state it might be willing to break new ground in directions that MUST felt important.

When the trustees met on February 20, they had a strong letter of endorsement from the student body, signed by the president of the student council and based on my conversations with them and the February 3 document. The faculty also responded, though only after very lengthy discussions. Several members of the faculty were very suspicious of my theological orientation. Those who had been a part of the old Biblical Seminary tradition had no confidence that its spirit would be maintained in any way. They were however, really caught in the situation where without a new president the seminary clearly could not function another year. At the moment there seemed to be no other choice, which led several members to support me with enthusiasm and others to feel that this was the only hope for the future. These memos from the students and from the faculty were read and discussed at the trustees' meeting along with several reports from alumni representatives who were very strongly against my election. The chairman of the board had also received a letter from Dr. Bonnell who, on the basis of the February 3 memo, wanted the trustees to know that he rescinded his endorsement of my candidacy and felt it would be a serious mistake to proceed. All this evidence was for naught, however, since the trustees once again clearly lacked a quorum and could not proceed with a legal election. When Mr. Midtbo explained this to me over the phone that evening, I suggested that it certainly underlined the comment in my report that the trustees were in a disaster situation and that they ought to close the seminary with as little pain and anguish as could be managed. He was, however, absolutely determined that the election would be managed and had arranged more or less legally for a special meeting of the board of trustees on March 3 for which they would seek absentee ballots from members who would not be present. When the trustees actually met on March 3, they had determined there were in fact twenty trustees. The actual vote was twelve for, three against, one abstaining, and four not voting. This was not exactly an overwhelming vote of confidence, but clearly the twelve votes had come from trustees who were deeply committed to the future. On learning that I would accept the assignment, several of the trustees decided to resign, as did one member of the faculty. With very mixed emotions, including a strong portion of anxiety, I undertook this new assignment on March 15, 1969.

It was obvious, however, that we were in a very special moment in theological education. Across the board, seminaries were asking hard questions about such issues as financing and trustee responsibility. During the years at Union the faculty rarely discussed such questions, but now patterns of teaching and curriculum, long taken for granted, were being reexamined. The future studies of the American Association of Theological Schools (AATS) were only one part of this time of ferment that also found expression in the restlessness of many seminary communities. The seminaries were on the threshold of two dramatic phenomena: the increase in the number of women students and the arrival of many more second-career students.

Although my commitments at Union and MUST were still heavy, I was able to spend two to three days a week in dealing with the three urgent tasks that confronted us: curriculum development, recruitment, and finances. A brief word about each:

Curriculum Development

Planning the curriculum for 1969–70. As I had indicated in the February 3 memo, it seemed to me that we needed to pay major attention to implementing at the master of divinity level the Curriculum for the Seventies. With nothing to lose, we ought to adapt as fully as possible to our own situation the suggestions in that document and give them the best possible trial. Here was the rationale that would justify the continuation of the seminary. At the same time, we would need to broaden our programs widely in order to attract a new constituency for the seminary, giving as the primary rationale our ability to equip men and women for ministry in an urban context.

Beginning on March 17, a planning committee of students and faculty, together with several trustees, met several times a week through June to give specific shape to the curriculum and to work out details for its implementation. We first came up with a goal statement that had been developed by a long-range planning committee. It read as follows:

> The purpose of New York Theological Seminary is to provide a community of learning in an urban setting, rooted in biblical encounter and commitment to Christ, which enables men and women to discover, and become equipped for, Christian living and mission in the contemporary world.

It was not easy to adapt the Curriculum for the Seventies. But drawing on that document we came up with the following presuppositions that needed to take shape in the specific elements of the curriculum:

1. We should live among those whom we are being educated to serve.
2. Our education should be fully ecumenical.
3. Our education should be associated with the continuing education of ministers and the training of the laity and should take place in study/action teams.
4. Our education should take advantage of existing institutions of higher education.
5. (We should have) access to persons with specialist knowledge.
6. Theology should be built upon the study of cultures and society.
7. Our education should be in integrated practical courses.
8. Our education must be geared toward specialist ministries.
9. We must be made aware of new techniques.
10. We must develop forms of worship that are worthy of the people of God.
11. Our education must be under constant evaluation and revision.
12. Authority and responsibility must be in the hands of both students and staff.

As the shape of the new program emerged, we developed a description that we could share with the trustees and that gave us a fairly clear picture of what we were about. We called this "Vision for a Seminary" and it looked like this:

VISION FOR A SEMINARY

The rationale for *reorienting* and *expanding* the program of New York Theological Seminary and a preliminary description of major components.

In calling a new president and making a determined effort to recruit a strong student body, finding new sources of funding and developing a challenging experimental curriculum, the trustees and faculty of New York Theological Seminary have made a fundamental commitment to a new future. Well aware that ecclesiastical institutions often live on far past the point of usefulness, we have been considering soberly the alternatives before arriving at the conviction that this seminary can play a unique, noncompetitive and vital role in theological education.

REORIENTATION:

At the bachelor of divinity and master of religious education levels we are structuring a curriculum along the lines of the proposal for seminaries developed for the American Association of Theological Schools by a committee of which Bill Webber was a member. This curriculum, seeking to relate reflection and involvement, focusing on a partnership in learning among faculty and students, and providing access to the educational resources of New York City, promises to be helpful to seminaries across the country. Our unique combination of urban location, ecumenical character, and ecclesiastical independence encourages us to undertake this exciting experiment.

EXPANSION:

At the same time, we plan to develop two major programs in areas that usually are seen to be somewhat tangential by traditional seminaries: (1) continuing education for clergy and (2) theological education for laity. Our vision for the future places the New York Theological Seminary in a servant relationship to three major constituents: the seminaries in this country, but in particular those in the metropolitan areas that are seeking to join in a new association; the clergy of the metropolitan area who seek continuing education; and the churches of this area who need the resources of theological schools in equipping their laity for mission and ministry.

In brief outline, these are the major components which we seek to expand or implement by the fall of 1969:

I. Programs at the BD and MRE levels

A. Experimental BD curriculum: Beginning in September, the seminary will institute for all entering students its version of the AATS "Curriculum for the Seventies." This will allow for great freedom in course selection and for students to proceed along lines of their own interest, taking advantage of the tremendous opportunities in New York City. The key to the program will be placement in a basic group of ten students and one faculty member representing one of the traditional disciplines. The style of the group will involve students and faculty as participants in a common learning experience, seeking to relate a key element of urban life and the insight and perspective of the biblical tradition. This kind of curriculum seems essential for the future. We hope that our efforts to implement the curriculum will serve as a guidepost for many other seminaries in the years ahead.

B. Metropolitan Intern Program: This program, developed by MUST, is designed to provide theological students with the experience of an intern year in New York City, either between college and seminary, or during seminary. This is a tested program that belongs under the direction of a seminary and is already operational. We expect approximately forty students to be enrolled in four units by September 1969.

C. Urban Ministry Term: We are offering seminaries all over the country either a semester or a year when their students may enroll with us for a term of work focused specifically on mission and ministry in the urban setting.

D. Joint Courses in Urban Ministry: We have already developed the first such course in cooperation with Union, Maryknoll and General seminaries. We are prepared to coordinate a variety of such joint courses on behalf of the Metropolitan Association of Theological Schools. Staff for such courses would be drawn from all the cooperating faculties.

II. Continuing Education for Clergy

As a basic pattern of service to this metropolitan area and to sister seminaries, we propose that under the umbrella of the Metropolitan Association of Theological Schools and in cooperation with MUST, New York Theological Seminary undertake continuing education that involves on-the-job training and missionary action.

A. STM Degree in Urban Ministry: The ground has been broken in this area by a cooperating program with MUST. It is now ready to be made operational on a much larger scale. In a three-year program, demanding approximately one full day a week, a parish clergyperson is challenged to excellence in practice of the ministry.

B. STM Degree in Pastoral Counseling: This program, like the program in urban ministry, is a form of on-the-job training in the pastoral counseling office. This is a one day per week (Wednesday) program lasting two academic years. It is conducted jointly with the Post-Graduate Center for Mental Health in New York City. Clergy of the three faiths can be accommodated.

C. Practical Theology for Young Pastors: We are proposing to the ecclesiastical judicatories that they encourage students in their first few years of parish assignment to devote one full period of twenty-four hours each week to continuing education, relating theological study to their practice of the ministry.

D. Continuing Education for Non-Degree Candidates: An urgent need, the details for which must be worked out in cooperation with the black and Puerto Rican communities, suggests a training program leading to a certificate for storefront pastors and other clergy who are not presently eligible for degree work. We are prepared to explore how to integrate such clergy into regular courses (for the sake of all concerned) as well as to develop special courses for their particular needs. Such a program demands new staff, local initiative, and considerable flexibility.

III. Theological Education for the Laity

Here again, on behalf of the seminaries in this area, we are prepared to implement a program of serious theological study for laity. This would require cooperative staffing and programs designed to fit the schedules of laity. Programs would be intended for serious students, with particular emphasis on relating faith to vocation and action.

A. Semester Academic Programs: We are prepared in the fall to develop a program of the churches on Manhattan's East Side as the first step in lay education. A preliminary program, the Lay School of Mission Theology, developed by MUST, has provided good experience and insight.

B. Community Based Schools of Theology for Laity: In the immediate future we suggest that a number of strategic suburban communities be consulted in terms of developing local programs of serious theological study, using the resources of all the cooperating seminaries.

C. Urban Training for Roman Catholic Nuns: We have already trained half a dozen nuns who seek insight into urban problems. A number of others are actively searching for urban training opportunities. In cooperation with MUST, we have a unique location and experience to meet this challenge.

CONCLUSION:

Most of these programs have already been tested to some degree and can be implemented in the fall of 1969, if:

1. We have gained the cooperation and support of the seminaries in this metropolitan area. As of this writing, we have the encouragement of Union, Drew, Princeton, General, and Maryknoll.
2. We can find competent people to staff these programs. The evidence is clear that we can hope not only to draw on the help, to some degree, of other seminaries, but that we have available in this metropolitan area an amazing reservoir of competent teachers in denominational jobs, parishes, and secular positions.
3. We have funds to meet the challenge.

Recruitment

The second urgent priority was recruitment. The seminary had depended for its student body on two primary sources. There were loyal alumni who would encourage men and women who sought their advice to consider their alma mater with its remarkable tradition of a biblically-centered curriculum. There were also a number of students who were based in the New York area who either did not want to leave the city or found that it was advantageous to attend a low-cost school to which they could commute.

This was the height of the Vietnam war as well as the civil rights movement. A great many college students were unclear about their vocational future and needed time to clarify their own values or simply to avoid the draft. Thus nondenominational seminaries attracted many people who had not yet made a clear commitment to ministry. There had also come out of the civil rights and war protest days a number of students who were looking for a somewhat unconventional educational opportunity. Thus for a variety of reasons, a seminary in the heart of New York City promising an experimental curriculum that focused on the education of students rather than on the teaching of disciplines caught the attention of a wide range of students in colleges and universities that had never sent students to Biblical Seminary. In April, I had written a letter to all the college professors and chaplains whom I knew across the country urgently requesting support for our recruiting efforts. It read in part as follows:

To College Professors and Chaplains:

This is a plea for help. After a long struggle, I have just accepted the presidency of New York Theological Seminary (formerly Biblical Seminary). The decision was made only after long negotiation and discussion with faculty, student body, and trustees. I could see no point in working to maintain and develop another small Protestant seminary.

A clear commitment has been made to press forward with educational experimentation and the kind of innovation that more traditional schools cannot easily undertake. Further, the combination of superb location in the heart of New York City, a small but really able faculty, and the freedom to experiment with education for ministry in an urban society, makes for an exciting challenge.

My plea is for your help in calling your students' attention to this kind of educational opportunity. I'm obviously not asking for any endorsement. But we are willing to guarantee to students a seminary program that takes their education with ultimate seriousness and a faculty committed to a new pattern of theological education, rather than the traditional scholar-teacher model.

We are not competing with either the denominational seminary or schools like Union or Yale Divinity. Rather, we shall seek to provide an experimental alternative to these traditional patterns and work at patterns of education that can break new ground for theological education. As a starting point, we are adapting to our situation and competence the basic ideas of the "Curriculum for the Seventies" developed by the AATS.

I would be glad to correspond or meet with any students who would like to explore this kind of graduate education. I believe we can give them an exciting and challenging program.

Faithfully yours,
George W. Webber
President

Finances

The third major priority was finances. A crisis came in early June when Mr. Midtbo, chairman of the board of trustees, walked into the office with a desperate look in his eyes to say that we would shortly run out of money and that he doubted we would be able to pay the bills through the summer. Although he was grateful for the energy that had been invested in planning for the future, he felt it was time to throw in the towel. Well aware of the financial crunch, I was not too surprised by his visit. When I had been considering the presidency, I had asked about seminary funds and was informed that it had an endowment of approximately $500,000. However the balance sheet revealed no invested funds. It turned out that the endowment was held in the form of a mortgage on the seminary's property, the result of the need to fund a payment for urgent capital expenses and the yearly deficits. I suggested to Mr. Midtbo that he take a good look at what it would cost to terminate the seminary before the fall term of 1969. It would be necessary to arrange for faculty terminal payments, alternative education opportunities for the students, and all the closing down expenses. He came back about an hour later with an estimate of at least $125,000. We both recognized that the projected deficit for the academic year was $10,000 more. With that we came to the common conclusion, shortly to be accepted by the trustees, that we would begin the academic year with a clear announcement to faculty and students that we intended to close at the end of the 1969–70 academic year unless two conditions had been clearly met: 1) we had developed an impressive curriculum, making a significant contribution to the theological education enterprise; and 2) we had in hand sufficient funds to pay for the current academic year and a clear prospect of functioning with a balanced budget in the next several years. With that the only question remaining was where to find the cash to pay our current bills!

It happened that the Broadway United Church of Christ had just made a large sale of property and had a great deal of cash on hand. They were agreeable to a loan at market interest. This enabled us to enter the year knowing that we could survive until decisions about the future were made and that the seminary did possess assets of considerable value in terms of its property in the heart of the city.

It was imperative that we find new funds from sources that were previously not available to the seminary. Throughout the years in East Harlem and even at MUST, I had been involved extensively in fund-raising responsibilities and set out to look for support from sources that had previously been helpful. I remember thinking that there was no time to build a broad base of financial support nor did I know wealthy individuals who might be cultivated. Rather there was a small handful of foundations that had some interest in theological education. The only viable hope was to focus on these, giving them almost all the fund-raising time available. By September this had resulted in a substantial grant of $30,000 from the Charles E. Merrill Trust and $15,000 from the Calder Foundation, but not much else was on the horizon.

Other Matters Needing Attention

In addition to these three major priorities (curriculum development, recruitment, and finances) there were several other matters that needed attention. One was the recruitment and morale of the trustees. By the May meeting, three of the older trustees had either resigned or asked not to be reelected. The statutes of the seminary called for thirty-six trustees. Now, with only twelve slots filled, it was quite simple to look for new trustees that would clearly support new directions and initiatives—what a blessing for a new president. The nominating committee recommended new members who were committed to the unfolding vision of the seminary and, in several cases, old friends. All of them had been long involved in the ministry in New York City and included Henry Pitney Van Dusen, the retired president of Union Theological Seminary; David Barry, president of the New York City Mission Society; Cal Gersten, a Lutheran layman, who was head of Christian Herald Charities; and Carl Fields, an educational consultant with remarkable skills in organizational development who had once been the trainer for the MUST staff. The result was a group of trustees committed to helping us develop a future for the seminary and committed to its emerging goals while still determined to honor the best part of the past. The bylaws were also changed to add three voting members from the faculty, three voting members from the alumni, and one from the student body.

Another problem that needed attention was that of the alumni. Many of the men and women who had studied at Biblical Seminary had maintained a fierce loyalty to their alma mater and were very suspicious of the developments in the sixties and even more so with a new president who was from Union. I made early efforts to meet with groups of alumni, inviting several hundred who lived in the New York metropolitan area to any one of four meetings held at various times. No more than six showed up at any session, but I did discover a number of persons, respected by other alumni, who offered genuine support, including Sam Wiley, the dean of General Theological Seminary, Nelle Morton of Drew Theological Seminary, and Sy Mack, long on the staff of the National Council of the Churches of Christ in the U.S.A. Dean Wiley's pungent advice was simple. "Don't lie to us like your immediate predecessors about the health of the seminary."

One further area of concern was faculty morale. The salary

level at the seminary had been woefully low for many years; this situation had not been helped by the fact that the half-time president had received a salary double that of the senior full professor. The issues of remuneration were dealt with as best as we could; we sought to place the salary of the president more in line with those of the rest of the faculty and to provide some modest raises. I was determined that the new curriculum would be made to work using the present faculty. They had solid graduate degrees and were most eager to help bring to reality what had come to be a shared vision of a new and exciting seminary life. For me, the task was to transform the seminary rather than to assume that the new curriculum would require a totally new faculty.

One happy event was my discovery of a biography of Wilbert Webster White, *The Bible in the Making of Ministers*, written by a grateful alumnus, Charles R. Eberhardt. Here, to my relief, I discovered the spirit of a man willing to take risks, committed to finding new patterns of education for ministry, and not dogmatic in his theology or fundamentalist in his biblical orientation. At one point he was quoted as stating, "If a person knows the scriptures, I'll trust their theology to the Holy Spirit." Armed with this new acquaintance with the thinking of Dr. White himself, I was now equipped to deal with skeptical alumni. I had a clear sense that we were trying in 1969 to find new wineskins for many of the commitments and concerns that had been expressed by Dr. White. Although the seminary was going to look different, I could hope that it might very well be informed by the same spirit. Our commitment as the core faculty to a strong biblical emphasis provided a vital link to the past.

At the same time, it was apparent that a number of faculty were highly suspicious of the new president. They were uncertain about how he was going to function in terms of shared authority, to what degree he would impose his own will and ride roughshod over them as had sometimes occurred in the past, and to what degree he would function primarily as a potent center of authority. It was John Kildahl, with his strong training in psychotherapy, who suggested it would be healthy for the faculty to spend some days away together, using an outside consultant who could help us look at our own relationships and develop a sense of mutual trust and solidarity. This was actually done in April, 1969, in a three-day visit at the continuing education center at Princeton Seminary. We used the resources of a Lutheran pastor from western Pennsylvania whom none of us had known personally before. It was an incredibly valuable time. Barriers fell, both old ones that had existed among some members of the faculty and new ones that had been erected by the faculty to defend themselves from the new president. This was a vivid reminder of the importance of giving attention to human relationships if an organization is to function with any kind of effectiveness, not least of all in a Christian organization.

By the end of June the details of the new curriculum had been worked out. Administrators had been hired to direct a program of lay studies and for the continuing education circle of our three-ring model. In both cases, their employment was an indication of what was to come. Both were hired on a part-time basis with the expectation that they would continue other commitments in ministry while fulfilling their administrative role at the seminary. The lay program was directed by Willis Elliott who came to the seminary after some years as a pastor, teacher, and then as staff for evangelism and church extension with the Board for Homeland Ministries of the United Church of Christ. The program in continuing education was directed by Melvin Schoonover who had been a colleague of mine in the East Harlem Protestant Parish and more recently had served as pastor of Chambers Baptist Church in East Harlem. Another fortuitous appointment was that of Bill Weisenbach, a graduate of the Class of 1969, as assistant to the president. He proved to be an invaluable source of wisdom and support. The prospects of a dramatically increased enrollment were apparent. The loan for $125,000 from Broadway United Church of Christ had been secured. And all of us with a certain amount of genuine anticipation and not inconsiderable anxiety looked forward to a new academic year.

In September 1969, a chaotic but fascinating year began with the arrival of a far larger entering class than the seminary had seen for many years. There were thirty-seven students in the entering MDiv class compared to a total of twenty-one in the second and third year group combined. A wide range of new programs was underway in response to our planning in the spring. A progress report was made available to our trustees soon after registration had begun:

> On March 3, 1969, the trustees and faculty of New York Theological Seminary in selecting a new president made a dramatic commitment to bring to reality a new vision of what a theological seminary must be and do. For some years, both the size of the student body and the available financial support had dwindled badly. Only a very radical program, urgent for the churches, authentically pioneering in theological education, and able to attract first-rate students could justify any attempt to restore validity and vitality to this institution. Such a program was given shape in late March under the heading "Vision for a Seminary" and has provided the mandate for intensive work in the subsequent months.
>
> The vision contained two basic assumptions: (1) that students in a theological seminary were mature men and women who must be trusted to engage in solid and relevant study as partners in a learning community; (2) that faculty members, accustomed to traditional models of professor, lecturer, scholar could effectively embrace a new style of teacher-student relationship, one marked by partnership and collegiality in learning. In other words, students will have a good deal of freedom in developing their program of study and involvement.
>
> In the actual programs of the seminary, we have made a radical departure from traditional seminary education which gives primary attention to training future clergy and teachers. At NYTS the new emphases were directed primarily to the continuing education of clergy, to lay training, and responding to the theological needs of the churches in the metropolitan area. Major opportunities include:
>
> 1. Training men and women for all types of Christian ministry through a vital new curriculum—this will capitalize on our unique urban location and will also provide a wide range of opportunities for men and women from other seminaries to work here for a year, semester, or summer;

2. Continuing education for hundreds of clergy, Catholic and Protestant, who desperately need a new understanding of the pastoral task and the role of the church in urban life;
3. A top-level series of schools of theology for laity in the metropolitan area as part of the Metropolitan Center of Lay Theological Study at the seminary.

In each of these programs, as they now take explicit shape during the current term, we are always about a task of interaction. Quite simply, we want to break the frequent dichotomy between academic studies and concrete experience; between theoretical disciplines and practical ones. In the past it has been too easy to treat biblical studies, church history, and theology as a vast body of knowledge that a student needed to master before he (she) could function as a professional. Our attempt is to develop a style of education in which theological study and concrete involvement in a sector of contemporary life will be in constant dialogue and interaction. The problem of black power, for example, raises fundamental issues for mission and ministry that require hard theological study, even as biblical faith produces a perspective with which to deal with racial injustice. This ability to relate faith to life, theology to practice, is the substance of a theologically trained person.

We have now on hand a remarkable group of entering students . . . larger than the combined number of the upper two classes. Three excellent programs in continuing education are underway and three lay schools of theology will begin shortly. The vision is becoming a reality.

Two issues remain dominant: we must engage in solid evaluation that will give us an honest picture of the validity and importance of our dream now that it is becoming operational, and we must find the resources for the next three years of operation while we build the broad base of continuing support that our task demands.

George W. Webber

While the continuation of the STM program for parish clergy provided both the continuity with the recent past and helpful funds, the major attention of the faculty was taken up with launching the seminary version of the "Curriculum for the Seventies." The first week of the semester was a "Time of Beginnings," designed to introduce the students to the process of creating a strong sense of community.

Partly to deal with my own anxiety, I had sent out a memo to faculty and students in August reminding them that we were determined to create a new pattern of relationships that would require considerable readjustment on the part of nearly everyone. Here was the clearest break with the patterns of Dr. White and Biblical Seminary. Students, faculty, administration, and trustees were seeking a pattern of mutual accountability and collegiality that was in sharp contrast to a hierarchical structure, with the trustees and president in charge, the faculty as employees, and the students as clients. The memo read in part:

> *In terms of curriculum, we have sought to free up the pattern of specific course requirements in favor of a style that sets clear goals of achievement but allows wide flexibility in arriving at them. In terms of seminary authority, we have devised a senate that has responsibility for basic policy and is made up of faculty and students in equal numbers. In terms of important elements of common life as a seminary body, we have left many decisions to be made in the fall when you can also be part of the process of final determination.*
>
> *The implementations of all this are, at best, a situation which can foster creative study, involvement, and maturity. At worst, we have devised a program fraught with potential for misunderstanding, confusion, uncertainty, and ambiguity. At many points, you will ask for policy only to find that we are in the process of making it. You will want answers to obvious questions of classes and schedules and then will discover that no one seems to have made any clear decision. Hopefully, this is an exciting context for learning, but I can only pray that you know, in some dim way, what you are getting into by coming in September to New York Theological Seminary.*

Each of the entering students was assigned to a basic core group that would meet weekly for an extended session and would provide the basic coordination of each student's educational experience. Here the students would integrate the various elements of their field work and study, give attention to their own faith pilgrimage, and, it was hoped, discover and experience the reality of an intentional Christian community. These groups of eight to ten students were led by a member of the full-time academic faculty.

The decision had been made to foment the community building process by submitting each of the core groups to a "marathon" session during the Week of Beginnings. The core group would meet for a gruelling session beginning in the afternoon and continuing through the night. With the help of an outside trainer, the purpose was to bring the group to a level of mutual understanding and trust that would enable them to work together effectively. The resistance this created was the first sign that the year would be exhausting and difficult. An unusual diversity of students from a wide range of religious traditions had arrived, a group not likely to find any curriculum uniformly acceptable. Almost none of the core groups found it easy to develop effective patterns. Where the students discovered a sense of community, the faculty person tended to be out of sync.

For many of the students, the curriculum began to offer exciting new learning possibilities. But for many of the faculty it was frustrating. Since there was ample opportunity for the students to voice their discontent in occasional evaluation sessions as well as in the student senate and directly to the president, I began to hear discontent about the faculty. It seemed that several of the faculty were very upset that the students did not seem interested in doing serious study or following through on suggested assignments. As a consequence, these faculty reverted to the authority patterns to which they had been accustomed.

The students were better able to adjust to the new situation than the faculty. In October they raised the issue of a moratorium day to work for peace in Southeast Asia. The faculty had given the senate, made up of both students and faculty, the right to make important decisions and felt themselves badly outvoted on the decision to have a moratorium day. On the scheduled day a large part of the student body participated in demonstrations with students from other seminaries. Students had also painted on the flat roof of the seminary a large dove as a peace symbol; it was in bright colors clearly visible from the upper floors of all the surrounding office buildings and it remained there as long as the seminary was located on 49th Street.

From my early days in East Harlem, I had always felt an obligation to keep careful records. We were involved in an experiment whose results, both positive and negative, needed to be reported and carefully examined. Thus at the beginning of the summer of 1969, the trustees and I agreed to secure the half-time services of a retired social scientist, Anne Fried, to monitor the development of the new curriculum and to provide for a steady process of evaluation and refinement. By early December, Dr. Fried had in hand a very long and extensive document that included evaluations of the individual courses taught by faculty members as well as a discussion of the effectiveness of the core groups, the morale of the community, and the responses of individual students and faculty. But in a private meeting with me she reported that, while she hoped her material would be helpful, she really had lost heart for the assignment and was resigning. She indicated that her affection for the faculty made it really unpleasant to paint the picture with the harshness that candor demanded! She had concluded that a competent faculty of trained scholar/teachers could not be expected to shift gears so dramatically and adopt such demanding new patterns of pedagogy. Nor did she feel it was really legitimate to ask this of them.

Fortunately, due to our funding crises we did not have to face the painful mismatch between the faculty and the new curriculum. The trustees had determined to close the seminary at the end of 1969 unless both an impressive curriculum was in operation and adequate future funding was secured. By December it had become quite apparent that the major foundations with interest in theological education were not about to support a property-poor seminary struggling for survival. The *coup de grace* came when I had a long conversation with Yorke Allen, an old friend and long-time supporter who was an executive for the Sealantic Foundation. This was the vehicle through which John D. Rockefeller Jr. had made available nearly $25,000,000 to strengthen theological education. It was the most obvious source of funding for any significant seminary venture. But Allen, while treating me with sympathy and graciousness, made it quite clear that from his perspective and that of his trustees it made no sense to help a seminary that was in such desperate straits and seemed to have no real potential for a strong future. But he thoughtfully suggested that I ask the chairman of the seminary board of trustees to talk with him so those responsible for the seminary had a first-hand picture of the attitude of potential funding sources. Mr. Midtbo came back from his long conversation with Allen quite shaken by the facts with which he had been confronted and the bleak picture he had been shown. I gather Allen said something to the effect that "I have supported Bill Webber in a variety of projects over twenty-five years, but this time he has taken on an impossible if not ridiculous task. I think the seminary needs to know that, from where I sit, there seems no likelihood of significant funding from any responsible foundation sources."

That day, the chairman of the board and I came to the recognition that, however exciting had been the curriculum, there was simply no way to continue funding the seminary. In light of our agreement made the previous June, we determined to recommend, when faculty and students returned from Christmas vacation, the closing of the seminary at the end of the academic year.

This we did to the shock of the student body and the alarm of the faculty. A trustee meeting had been scheduled for January where a decision would be made in light of the earlier agreements. In Anne Fried's survey, over two-thirds of the students had indicated their general enthusiasm for the year in spite of their frustrations with the faculty, and their clear commitment to return if the seminary were indeed open. In nearly every case they agreed to recommend the seminary to friends who were interested in theological education. So they were dismayed at the prospect of the closure of an institution that had provided them with such freedom and opportunity. The faculty for their part were well aware that jobs in seminary and college religion teaching were scarce and that they would have a very difficult time finding other employment. It was an anguishing time for the president who had to propose the closure. And while I never feared for my personal safety, it was certainly a highly charged and unpleasant atmosphere.

On the day of the trustees' meeting there was a mass rally of faculty and students to plot their strategy for dealing with the trustees and finding a way to survive. When the trustees met, I urged them to open the meeting to anyone who wished to attend, which they gladly did. So when most of the faculty and a large number of the students knocked on the door, they were welcomed with a word from the chair to the effect that they were colleagues in the task and that the board of trustees had no desire to close this institution and that certainly he did not, but they simply had been unable to find an alternative. Students and faculty with one voice insisted that there must be a way to continue and requested a month's time to come up with alternatives for survival. On this basis, the trustees agreed to postpone any action, but with the understanding that the faculty could not count on contracts for the coming year.

Thus began six weeks of very great travail for all of us. All kinds of alternatives were proposed, most of which assumed a fairly drastic reduction in faculty, which would almost certainly mean loss of accreditation. To reduce costs in other ways than that simply could not be imagined. The struggle went on during a faculty retreat, many meetings of the seminary senate, and a variety of consultations. None of the proposed alternatives seemed to offer any hope of a solution. The only radical suggestion that emerged was in a letter from Willis Elliott, employed the previous summer as director of our lay program, to his faculty colleagues, suggesting that the fundamental financial problem arose from the heavy percentage of the budget that was devoted to faculty salaries. He suggested that they resign *en masse*. While this met with resistance and occasionally with anger from the faculty, it did drop a seed in my mind. This germinated in a memo that I sent to the students and faculty three days before the March trustee meeting. In it I suggested that if we were to stop offering the full three-year master of divinity (then BD) program in which we were in competition with other seminaries and which created an enormous expense, we would then have the opportunity and the right to terminate the contracts of the entire faculty. This seemed a lot healthier than terminating some while maintaining others, since those who were not retained would have even greater difficulty securing a position than if they could say that the entire faculty had been terminated. Such action could free us to provide a different educational profile that would include continuing education programs for laity and a year of contextual urban education for MDiv students from seminaries around the country. The situation came to a head on March 12 at a meeting that began at 5:15 in the afternoon and did not adjourn until nearly 10:00 that night. Again it was open to students and faculty as well as the voting members of the board. The suggestion that the seminary continue with a reduced faculty was voted down after long discussion. Several alternative proposals also seemed to offer no solution. But a motion to close the seminary at the end of the academic year and sell off the assets and make them available to continue solid biblical education in other seminaries nearly passed. What finally emerged followed the lines of my memo sent out three days earlier. The trustees voted to terminate the bachelor of divinity three-year program, thus terminating all faculty contracts at the conclusion of the academic year, and then voted to continue the other programs that had been undertaken during that year and previously.

It was a long, hectic session. We had made a difficult and demanding decision that left me wondering how I had gotten into this and how I would proceed. Now the ball was clearly in my court with a whole rebuilding job to be undertaken. The mandate to terminate the full-time faculty did not apply to John Kildahl, who would continue his part-time direction of the pastoral counseling program, nor to Mel Schoonover, who could now take an even larger role in the continuing education circle. Moreover, I still had the support of Willis Elliott, who had been coordinating the program in lay education. The four of us composed what we now called the administrative faculty—1970–71 was in our hands.

The board had the good sense to make very generous terminal arrangements with the faculty, promising them twelve months of full salary and benefits at the completion of their current contracts less any income they might secure from new positions. In retrospect this was a great step, far more generous than might have been expected given the financial situation of the seminary and the understanding nine months earlier that there would probably be no new contracts at the end of the current year. As a matter of fact, one member of the faculty helped us with a personal loan during the summer. I think the others, while put in somewhat difficult circumstances by the decision, recognized that there was no alternative and that it was better to terminate the entire group than to retain a few.

By March 17, less than a week later, we had been able to describe the basic rudiments of the coming year. With the help of the chair of the board of trustees, we could foresee the year's financing with the expectation of a balanced budget. To the chair it somehow seemed impossible, but the figures looked reasonable enough.

In order to clarify our situation, we provided the trustees with the following statement called "A Commitment to the Future":

> On March 12, 1970, the Trustees of New York Theological Seminary voted to:
>
> 1. Continue an experimental program of theological education which will be concentrated in a one-year program for BD students;
> 2. Discontinue, after a transitional year, the three-year BD program and the two-year MRE program, granting the last degrees in May, 1971;
> 3. Continue the program in both continuing education and lay education as well as the metropolitan intern program.
>
> The decision to substitute a one-year specialized program for the traditional three-year BD program was made for two reasons. The first was that it had become economically impossible to find the resources to maintain the accredited three-year BD program. The second reason was to place New York Theological Seminary in a truly noncompetitive situation with other seminaries by concentrating—in a one-year program—on our more unique contributions to theological

> education and service to other seminaries. The new program will be carried on with part-time faculty.
>
> The trustees have also affirmed that the new experimental program for BD students will be based on the seminary's unique urban location and its strong commitment, as set forth in its statutes, to a curriculum solidly rooted in biblical study. In the new curriculum a two-foci educational pattern is envisioned in which involvement in responsible ministry/action/service is balanced with solid theological study centered in a commitment to biblical study in depth. Theological education for this year is thus a process of interaction between traditional theological disciplines and the realities of contemporary life, between biblical faith and social responsibility, between theology and practice in the Christian life. The suggestion for this style of education came from the same "Curriculum for the Seventies" developed by the American Association of Theological Schools but modified by our experience in the present academic year.

It was determined that we would operate on something like a piece-work basis in terms of faculty salaries; that is, putting a price on each of the administrative and academic functions that needed to be undertaken. For example, the dean of lay theology slot paid $5,000; each course in a degree program paid $1,800; a lay theology course $1,000. The total stipend was determined by adding up the pay for each person's assignments. There was no tenure. Contracts for all were on a one-year basis. It was also expected that faculty would continue to have an active role in congregational ministry. The model was of an administrator-teacher-church person. For a person committed primarily to scholarly work and to teaching, NYTS was not a congenial environment.

One other increasingly significant development had to do with the role of Harold Midtbo, chair of the board of trustees during my first year. He had retired in the spring of 1969 as a top executive of Esso Eastern. A very articulate and committed Christian, caring very much for New York Theological Seminary, he had offered to make available two days a week of his time to assist the seminary in any way that would be helpful. His presence was a great gift at many levels. As a Lutheran with fifteen years involvement in the life of the seminary, he was trusted and respected by the older alumni including those with a very conservative theological bent. The fact that he was supportive of the developments at the seminary and was willing to put so much energy into helping it continue gave a validation to our work that otherwise would have been difficult to attain.

It also proved helpful to have an articulate, knowledgeable layperson who could raise questions for the faculty and administration that otherwise would not have occurred to us. Yet, it was a little unnerving for me to have the president of the board of trustees on hand two days a week, and it led to the possibility of considerable role confusion between us. I hit on the idea of electing an alumnus from the older days as chair of the board. While continuing as a member, Mr. Midtbo became the vice-president for financial administration and treasurer of the seminary. This meant that he would be working for me those two days of a week. As a businessman with experience in a large bureaucracy, he was quite willing to accept my leadership. It is true that from time to time when I did something that he felt was quite out of order, he would revert to being a trustee, but our relationship became one of remarkable mutual support and complementary functioning for the subsequent fourteen years.

As a footnote, it is worth reporting that most of the faculty found appropriate positions, often ones that were even more fulfilling than those at New York Theological Seminary and have continued to be sources of support and encouragement over the subsequent years. It was certainly a gift of grace that the drastic surgery did not lead to any obvious bitterness or recrimination. The faculty's very gracious acceptance of the inevitable made the transition far less painful than would have otherwise been the case.

CHAPTER 2

The Leading of the Spirit

Seeking to Live as a Pilgrim Seminary 1970–1975

The fall of 1970 had a feeling far different from that of a year earlier. In 1969 we were engaged with a large new student constituency, filled with anxiety and facing a very uncertain future, that had arrived to test a new curriculum. We had also had to seek massive new funding, in the awareness that if we were unsuccessful it might well have been the last year of the seminary. Now in September, 1970, there was the prospect of a future with the freedom to experiment, to try a variety of new programs, and to explore the needs of urban churches for the resources of a seminary. With a small administrative team, a much reduced budget, and no longer the inertia of a traditionally trained faculty, we had a sense of opportunity to develop, knowing now that if we failed, we would take responsibility and not blame the past. If during the first years, I had felt the freedom from feeling that nothing I did could make things worse, now there was the freedom in having no one to fault but myself. It was exhilarating for the small group of us,

Bill Weisenbach as assistant to the president, Mel Schoonover responsible for degree programs, Willis Elliott for work in lay education, and John Kildahl for pastoral counseling.

It became almost a weekly ritual for Harold Midtbo, who for fifteen years had struggled continually to keep the seminary afloat financially, to have the business manager produce a full financial report. He simply could not believe that we were actually making it, had funds in hand, and seemed almost certain to end the year with a balanced budget. This was due to a variety of factors. We no longer had a residential student body, and our part-time constituents, usually fully employed and already providing for their own board and room, could in most cases supply a significant amount of the modest tuition that their part-time programs required. In the second place, we were able to use over half of the total building space as an economic asset, renting the dormitory rooms to individuals who had some remote connection with the seminary or with a church and the larger office space to compatible nonprofit organizations that included during this period the Christian Herald Charities, an alcoholic rehabilitation program, Clergy and Laity Concerned, and Bread for the World. As a result, the building suddenly became a financial asset producing between $25,000 and $50,000 a year over and above its operational expenses.

Two other financial factors were also at work. In our new style the faculty was paid on a piecework basis with no full-time salaries necessary. For the most part they were expected to combine administration with teaching rather than to see themselves as scholars who did some teaching. Finally, once we had made the drastic alteration in our style and ventured on the pattern of new programs we found significant foundation support coming our way. The first breakthrough in the fall was a substantial grant for the Urban Year program from the Sealantic Foundation. This was a source of particular encouragement since the staff of that foundation examined rigorously all requests that came to their attention and the grant was a very significant affirmation of what we were about.

On another level, two sources of frequent tension in the academic community were largely eliminated. In our arrangement, the core teaching team consisted of five persons who came to be called the administrative faculty. These were the president, administrative assistant, and three deans.[1] By definition, administrators such as deans identify with the administration rather than with the faculty, who sometimes assume an adversarial relationship. All other faculty were part-time, employed as student needs required. At the same time, the board of trustees, made up largely of men and women who reflected the constituency of our programs, came to us as colleagues eager to share in uncovering new program patterns and to function more as partners than as the ultimate authority in our work.

The emerging program pattern for 1970–71 involved three components consisting of first degree or MDiv level education, continuing education for clergy, and lay theological education. The following diagram reveals that at a number of points, the programs overlapped resulting in considerable enrichment from putting together, in common learning situations, laity, clergy, and those preparing for ordained ministry. A number of classes were open to students from any of our programs, but with clearly differentiated requirements for academic credit. In retrospect, one fact stands out. All of these programs, with only one exception, were still designed for Christians in mainline denominations. The constituency of traditional accredited seminaries was still the target of both BD level work and our continuing education. Lay programs were aimed at the members of Catholic and Protestant parishes, largely white and middle class. Only slowly did we discover the presence of a large and eager new constituency in the black and Hispanic churches of the city.

The diagram reflects the dramatic change that was to come about over those five years. We continued to use the three-ring model as a way of visual description but the content underwent a startling change. A brief description of the programs in 1970–71 follows.

---

1. See Appendix B for biographical information on these members of the administrative faculty.

1970–71 PROGRAM PATTERN

I. Master of Divinity level
   A. Urban Year
   B. Metropolitan Intern Program

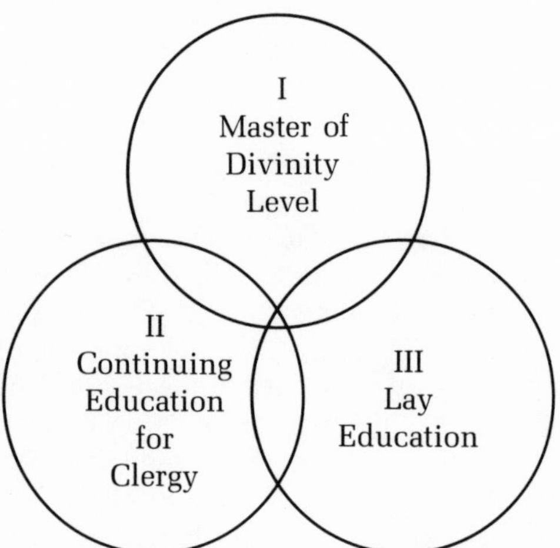

II. Continuing Education for Clergy
   A. STM in Pastoral Counseling
      1. Post-Graduate Center
      2. Lutheran Medical Center
   B. STM in Parish Ministry
      1. at NYTS
      2. Army Chaplain School
      3. Dispersed Groups

III. Theological Education
   A. Courses at NYTS
   B. Lay Centers in the Region
   C. Mid-career Exploration

By 1975–76, the pattern had evolved into this:

1975–76 PROGRAM PATTERN

I. Seminary (graduate level) Programs
   A. Doctor of Ministry (1974)
   B. STM Degrees:
      1. Pastoral Counseling
      2. Parish Ministry
   C. Master of Professional Studies
      1. Pastoral Counseling
      2. Parish Ministry
   D. MPS/MDiv (with New Brunswick) (1977)

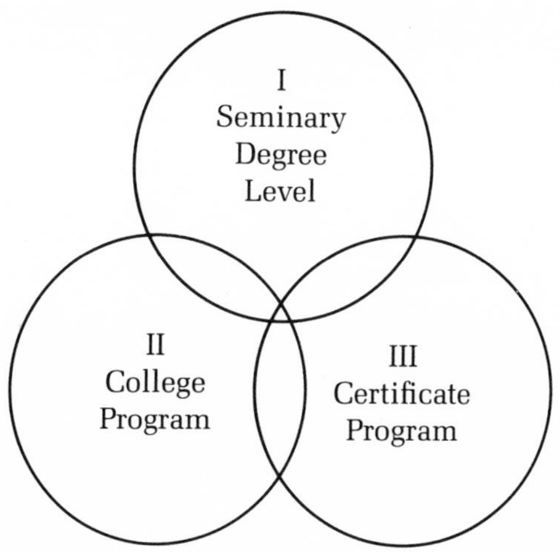

II. College Program
   A. Adelphi University (1973)
   B. College of New Rochelle (1975)

III. Certificates:
   English
   Hispanic

Program I: Master of Divinity Level Work

There were two main elements in this program:

A. The Metropolitan Intern Program. This program, as described earlier, provided students with the opportunity for a year of life in the city outside the academic environment. Each participant lived in an inner-city neighborhood and met there regularly with a unit of approximately ten students. During the year 1970–71, twenty-five students were enrolled in the program. In almost every instance there was clear evidence of remarkable growth in both personal maturity and vocational clarity. Union Seminary offered the program as a pre-seminary internship. For students from other seminaries across the country, it served as an internship after their first or second year in seminary. In either case, the student was protected from the draft but gained only modest credit toward a seminary degree.

B. The Urban Year. This was a one-year program taking the place of one of the three years required for a bachelor of divinity degree. It was open to students registered in any accredited seminary. It was designed to give major attention to the fundamental task of theological education enabling the Christian to understand the meaning and consequences of commitment to Jesus Christ. We called this "doing theology," that is, relating Christian faith and contemporary history, theology and practice, reflection and action. Equal amounts of time were devoted to study and to practice in some form of ministry with the aim of developing a style of interaction between knowledge from scripture and tradition on the one hand and from involvement in life as a Christian on the other.

   During the 1970–71 academic year, students were enrolled from six seminaries. Andover-Newton, Harvard, Princeton, General, Union, and Pittsburgh had guaranteed academic credit to their students. During 1971–72, following our example, Wesley Seminary also instituted such a program for a group of its own students.

Program II: Continuing Education for Clergy

This formed the second circle. Two of the major components had already been tested by the seminary during the previous three or four years.

A. Master of Sacred Theology in Pastoral Counseling. Here was our most established and efficient program. During 1970–71 nearly sixty clergy were enrolled in a degree program. This involved them in study each Wednesday from 9:30 to 3:30 under the direction of the Post-Graduate Center for Mental Health. During four academic terms they took 16 academic courses under excellent instruction. Each term in the afternoon they took one course at NYTS in the traditional theological disciplines. Other clergy were engaged at Lutheran Medical Center in Brooklyn. In every case, the goal was quite simple; to enable the parish pastor to gain skill and insight in counseling and group leadership. The program specifically was not to train full-time professional therapists, but rather to enhance the skills of the parish clergy person.

B. Master of Sacred Theology in the Practice of Parish Ministry. This second master's degree had been developed over the previous several years in connection with MUST. Its purpose was clear: to enhance the pastor's effectiveness in the practice of parish ministry. The basic components of the program were a series of four workshops, each occupying a full afternoon once a week. Our commitment was to provide a clear relationship between theology and practice. The program required a period of two years and in nearly every case provided the clergy with a rationale and the skills and confidence to develop greater effectiveness and integrity in the work of ministry.

C. Finally, we made our first attempt to provide continuing education for the countless storefront pastors and other inner-city clergy who served in our urban neighborhoods but did not possess advanced degrees. From the years in East Harlem as well as through modest efforts at MUST, I was well aware of the creative role such clergy often played in the life of their communities. During 1970–71, we offered programs for these clergy in three different neighborhoods, but without much success. The fact that it was largely at our initiative rather than a response to a clearly articulated need was part of the problem. In Bedford-Stuyvesant, for example, we worked over several semesters with a group of Pentecostal pastors. They wanted our help very specifically in dealing with institutions of government that overwhelmed their people, such as the departments of welfare and education and the criminal justice system. They also asked to pursue the question of how a biblical faith both requires and enables one to relate to such human problems as welfare, education, and housing that had traditionally been looked upon as secular, not religious, concerns.

Program III: Theological Education for Laity

The first component of this program includes courses for lay persons held both at the seminary and in a variety of neighborhoods in the greater New York area. From its beginning, the program aroused great interest and during 1970 nearly 300 persons registered in the various courses. They usually met for twelve weeks although sometimes only for half that time. Our purpose was clear: to offer serious theological study to lay persons who wanted to deepen their understanding of the Christian faith. Nearly all the courses tended to follow the style of interaction, that is, relating current issues and problems to theological tradition and scriptural insights. The program was made viable by the presence in the New York area of a large number of qualified teachers who seemed eager to accept the challenge of working with lay persons even for a very modest remuneration. I learned at one point that Gregory Baum would be studying for several years at the New School for Social Research not far from the seminary. We prevailed upon him to offer a Saturday morning course for lay persons. To his delight and our surprise, over eighty persons, including a high percentage of Roman Catholic nuns, became a most enthusiastic class and since we paid our faculty a percentage of the tuition, it proved to be very lucrative for him as well.

The second element in lay theological education was what was called initially "second career preparation" and eventually "mid-career exploration." We had been aware that many lay persons were seeking help in preparing for effective Christian service upon retirement or as an alternative career. At the same time we kept coming across lay persons who said something to the effect, "I have been going to church all my life. Unless I can find out what it means to be more intentional and serious about it, I've got better things to do on Sunday." The result was the inauguration in the fall of 1970 of a one-year program for ten men and women who met bi-weekly at the seminary for a long session plus an occasional weekend retreat. They had considerable flexibility in developing their own curriculum. The focus was on helping the persons in that particular group deal with issues of faith and vocation that were of concern to them. They were not unlike a "base community" as they sought to relate scripture and theology to the decisions and concerns of their lives.

The Programs Evolve

Five years later, the seminary programs were still defined by three overlapping rings, but their substance was vastly different. Typical was the failure of some of our projects and the emergence of quite new and unexpected challenges. It seems all too accurate to say that whenever we fashioned a new program that we thought would meet some very important need among clergy and laity in the New York area, and then sought to recruit for it, it almost always failed. Somehow the bright ideas which we dreamed up in the recesses of the seminary didn't take off. The programs that had by 1975 become the content of the three rings were for the most part those that came about when a group of persons laid before us very clear needs and demanded that we shape academic programs to meet them. It was more than a little humbling to realize that our own bright ideas didn't work very well, but it was also a source of gratitude to feel that we were being led by the Spirit to discovering new opportunities that we had not dreamed up ourselves.

One example makes the point. When we offered programs

in black communities for storefront clergy, the attendance was small and drizzled off quickly. When a group of inner-city clergy asked that we provide counseling training for them, an exciting new program developed.

The catalytic factor that changed the life of the seminary was the realization that in the black and Hispanic religious communities there was a vast and unmet need for serious education for ministry among the clergy and the laity. One had only to travel through any of the many inner-city neighborhoods in New York to discover the presence of hundreds of storefront churches, congregations meeting in former movie houses or synagogues, reflecting the ministries of independent Baptist, Holiness churches, and a variety of Pentecostal denominations. Here was the one indigenous form of community organization in the ghettos of the city. With no outside funding, meeting often five nights a week plus most of Sunday and often reflecting a vitality not usually found in the more affluent churches, these congregations were served almost exclusively by leaders who had not had access to higher education, either college or seminary. In the Hispanic community for instance, ministers of the Pentecostal churches were products of the Bible School education. It was our unexpected ability to respond to the needs of these clergy for education that formed the basis of the changes at NYTS.

No wonder, then, that trustees and faculty began to use the image of a pilgrim seminary. In the fall of 1974, several of the trustees grew anxious about the need to do a better job of planning for the future and at one meeting asked where I thought the seminary ought to be in five years. I told them that two years earlier we would have been totally unable to visualize what was in fact taking shape. Thus it hardly made sense to project the present very far into the future! Our hope was simply to remain open to the leading of the Spirit. Although we all recognized the necessity of long-range planning, descriptions of how our programs evolved may in retrospect illuminate how we did feel the leading of the Spirit, rather than our competence in such planning.

Simply put, the faculty learned to listen to the genuine needs and concerns of the students, to shape a curriculum in response, rather than to fit students into our design of a curriculum. The seminary needed to fit the student, rather than the student fit the seminary.

The diagram on pages 46–47 shows that Program I became the circle that included all seminary degree programs. Circle II, Continuing Education for Clergy, became a college degree for clergy and some lay persons. Circle III, Lay Education, became a Certificate Program largely for laity but also including a significant number of clergy. Probably the key to the unfolding program, in addition to our freedom to experiment, was the following commitment, "The task of New York Theological Seminary is to provide education for clergy and laity in the New York metropolitan area which will enable them to fulfill their calling more faithfully." Thus we were receptive to requests from a wide range of communities and greatly diverse needs.

CIRCLE I. This is the easiest of the seminary degree programs to describe. The STM programs in parish ministry and pastoral counseling continued, though with somewhat reduced numbers. It became obvious that there were many clergy who for a variety of reasons wanted to undertake the Doctor of Ministry program. Although we were convinced that the requirement for our STM, one full day per week of intensive study over a two-year period, was roughly equivalent in terms of demand to many of the doctor of ministry programs that were emerging around the country, we undertook our own doctor of ministry in the fall of 1974. This presupposed not only an MDiv degree but also our STM degree or its equivalent.

During this period, recruitment for the urban year program and the metropolitan intern both gradually dwindled. The intern year no longer was needed as a moratorium period as increasing numbers of college students took a year or more away during the college years. Further, the pressure of the war in Vietnam had also ended. For the urban year program, the loss of students reflected several realities. New York had become more and more a frightening place in the national image. Also, as an ever higher percentage of seminary students were married, it was difficult to uproot a family for one year in the midst of the three-year program.

But the voice of a new constituency was heard loudly and clearly and led us to inaugurate once again courses leading to a master of divinity degree. The decision in the spring of 1970 to terminate the MDiv degree had left us free from all the demands and requirements of this basic degree. However, we began to hear from many persons black, Hispanic, and white that their greatest need was for a master of divinity degree and that we had better create that opportunity again if we were serious about serving the needs of clergy and laity in the New York metropolitan area. Although we had no idea we could possibly mount the degree program once again, we stumbled by accident on a route to this goal. During Lent, 1974, I was invited to preach at a Wednesday service at the New Brunswick Theological Seminary. On the way into the chapel I asked the president if he would consider joining us in creating a master of divinity degree for minority students living in the New York metropolitan area. Several weeks later he called up to ask if I was serious. The result was a two-hour meeting in June during which we sketched out a pattern by which students would be recruited by New York Theological Seminary for an initial year of master of professional study, during which they would take a weekly four-hour introduction to the life and work of ministry and an equally demanding four-hour introduction to systematic theology. Those who could meet the academic requirements would then be accepted by New Brunswick as full MDiv level students. Together with New Brunswick, we would provide them with courses each Monday and Wednesday evening that would enable them over a four-year period, plus two intensive weeks in residence in New Brunswick each summer, to complete all the requirements for a fully accredited master of divinity degree. The discovery of New Brunswick once again represented more grace than planning. I had earlier sought the interest of both Union and General Seminary in examining the needs of minority leaders for MDiv education, but with no response. It turned out that New Brunswick Seminary had a dedicated faculty committed to the life of the church and willing to open themselves to the challenge of meeting the needs of a constituency far different from the white, male, Reformed Church students to whom they were accustomed.

The first group, in the fall of 1974, numbered seventeen. But this proved to be only the tip of an iceberg. In subsequent years it became apparent that there were a vast number of men and women, clergy and laity, in the New York metropolitan area who were desperate for such an evening program that would enable them to gain the credentials required for ordination in the mainline denominations. These were persons who could not leave their present family or professional or ecclesiastical responsibilities to attend a traditional residential seminary.

This period saw the emergence of a new degree not recognized by the Association of Theological Schools but urged upon us by the State Education Department: the master of professional studies. The need arose from the fact that a great many persons who were deeply committed to a religious vocation wanted the training provided by our STM in pastoral counseling or parish ministry. For example, many Roman Catholic nuns who had recognized college degrees and had been doing educational work for many years were now becoming parish assistants and were involved in social welfare services that required a wholly different set of skills. They did not want a master of divinity degree, but our STM program was exactly right for them. There were also many minority clergy who had been serving as pastors for many years who were seeking these two degrees but had no need for the master of divinity degree. Providing them with a seminary degree called master of professional studies in either pastoral counseling or parish ministry met a very great need and gained an immediate response. Since these students were mature men and women much involved in ministry, they found relatively little difficulty participating in the same workshops and seminars taken by students who were using the program for an STM degree.

Circle II. The development of this circle into an accredited college program was quite unexpected. The story goes back to 1972 and related to the decision of the Lutheran Medical Center in Brooklyn to remain in what had been a Scandinavian neighborhood but was now largely deserted by the original immigrants and was becoming increasingly a very densely populated black and Hispanic inner-city neighborhood. The hospital, having decided to remain, had the good sense to try to relate its activities to the local neighborhood and to hire a young Hispanic Pentecostal pastor to be its community relations staff person. Ray Rivera was an energetic pastor with many contacts in the neighborhood and was able to undertake his hospital work while continuing his church responsibilities. He was startled to discover the blond blue-eyed Lutheran seminary students who were doing clinical pastoral education in the hospital and wanted to know who they were. When he was informed that they were seminarians, seeking to gain pastoral skills by working in the hospital wards, he was quite upset. He informed the hospital chaplain that these Lutherans had no business trying to pastor to minority patients from totally different theological traditions. "Why," he asked, "doesn't the chaplain train minority clergy to work with their own people?"

This resulted in New York Theological Seminary providing the funds for an extended clinical pastoral education (CPE) quarter for Hispanic Pentecostal clergy. They spent a day-and-a-half each week in the hospital over a nine-month period and received what amounted to one-quarter of clinical training. This violated many of the canons of the clinical pastoral education establishment and provided a very startling challenge to the supervisors, who had to take seriously the unique student body with which they were suddenly presented.

Through this program, Ray Rivera came to know New York Theological Seminary and one day laid down a strong challenge: "Look, if Chaplain Jeasen can provide CPE for my clergy, you've got to provide them with theological education." I responded that we had tried hard to offer educational opportunities for Hispanic and black clergy without much success, but that if he would find twenty-five clergy who were ready for education and would have them fill out on sheets of paper their names, why they wanted education, and what kind of commitment they would make, I would be glad to talk further. I was soon invited to meet with a group of thirty men who insisted that we find a way to help them with their education. It became obvious that the need was not for graduate theological education. This group, all of them male, were lacking any college credentials and had not found in the city educational opportunities in any way relevant to their needs. What they required was a college liberal arts program that took them seriously as strong community leaders with maturity and competence in their own right, and, at the same time, provided them with an education that would equip them to fulfill more adequately their opportunities in ministry. Thus a course in politics would not be on Aristotle's political theory but on how New York City is governed. There would be courses on the sociology of the city. Literature courses would enable them to learn more about their own heritage and to read the literature of their own tradition as well as to read more broadly.

It was an exciting prospect and plans fell into place with remarkable rapidity. A phone call to the Lilly Endowment elicited a strong interest and within two weeks the pledge of funds sufficient to undertake a three-year program. Ray Rivera located an adult learning program through Adelphi University. And the staff there indicated their willingness to provide courses at the seminary. Within three months from the time Ray first brought up the matter, we were underway with our first group of twenty-five students equally divided between black and Hispanic church leaders. It was the beginning of a program that evolved from its initial period with Adelphi University to a try with Empire State College (the University Without Walls), and eventually, in the fall of 1975, landed with the College of New Rochelle, a small Roman Catholic women's college. The move to New Rochelle came out of desperation. Adelphi provided good instruction, but had little interest in dealing with state and federal funding sources that would have been available to most of the students. Frustrated, we turned to Empire State College, which offered courses through its University Without Walls. But this required largely independent study, which was not helpful to most of our students. They needed the discipline and stimulation of regular class sessions. Noting my travail with the program, one of the trustees, herself an Ursuline sister, suggested I try her college, New Rochelle. This proved to be a wonderful solution. The administration saw the creation of a branch campus at New York Theological Seminary as an appropriate part of the mission of the Ursuline sisters, who have provided a superb educational opportunity ever since. By the fall of 1975, nearly two hundred students were enrolled, attending classes that were mostly held in the evening. The banner you see as you enter the eleventh floor of the seminary facilities reads "The College of New Rochelle School of New Resources at New York Theological Seminary." Although the students are clearly registered through the college and will receive their AB from New Rochelle, many of them, when asked, would say they are attending New York Theological Seminary. It has been a most felicitous relationship between the college and the seminary.

CIRCLE III. By 1975, the final circle was the Certificate Program. The mid-career exploration program, after taking three groups of eight to ten students through a year-long program, was unable to recruit further. The lay classes at the seminary gradually dwindled in size, leading us to some serious evaluation as to why this no longer seemed to be a desired offering. Nothing we tried, including new and imaginative staffs, aroused the interests of lay persons in taking extensive courses on 49th Street. Meanwhile, however, a dramatic change had taken place in what had begun as a continuing education program for black clergy in several urban neighborhoods. The Christian Church (Disciples of Christ), located in Indianapolis, was closely related to a black denomination called the Churches of Christ, Disciples of Christ with many congregations in the New York metropolitan area. For these black clergy ordination was based on evidence of a clear call to ministry and did not require any formal theological education. But their bishops had prevailed on the sister denomination to provide funds for continuing education for the clergy. New York Theological Seminary was asked to take responsibility for this. During two semesters, an enthusiastic group of laity and clergy, numbering sixty on an average, gathered each Saturday for morning and afternoon sessions. This was on-the-job training at its best. Most of the success of the program was due to the leadership of Robert Washington, newly appointed to the administrative faculty as Dean of Black Studies. As a lay person, he was better able to move across denominational lines than a clergy person, who would be seen as representing one element of the black church community. Nor was he seen as a competitor by black clergy.

His imagination stirred by the response in Brooklyn, Dean

Washington decided that he would attempt the same kind of program for black church leaders to be held at the Seminary. This we called our certificate program. It was offered for twenty-eight weeks during the academic year, each Saturday beginning about 9:00 in the morning and continuing until 3:00 in the afternoon. We were utterly amazed that by the second year of the program one hundred students were registered with seventy-five to eighty in attendance every week and ten or fifteen of that number having 100 percent attendance. It is almost unbelievable that men and women, who for the most part are involved in full-time secular jobs and in the life of local congregations, would be so anxious for education that they would come for a full Saturday over a whole academic year. This kind of faith/commitment and eagerness for learning provided the teachers with an exciting challenge. We never had any difficulty recruiting faculty to teach in the certificate program.

Shortly after the initiation of this English-language program, made up almost exclusively of black laity and clergy, Jose Caraballo was appointed dean of the Hispanic Program at New York Theological Seminary. Caraballo had been a member of the first college courses taught under Adelphi and was the first to receive the bachelor's degree. He had for some years pastored a church of the Assembly of God, Eastern District. He had also played a variety of leadership roles in this the largest of the Pentecostal denominations. But before coming to the Seminary he had worked for the New York Bible Society in a post that took him regularly into a large proportion of the Hispanic congregations of every denomination in the metropolitan area. He quickly determined that a certificate program should also be available to Hispanic clergy and laity. However, he faced a unique problem. The primary vitality in the Hispanic community in the New York area lies in the Pentecostal churches. Every new member in a Pentecostal church is expected to attend one of their indigenous Bible schools for two and often three years. Thus a very extensive education program was available for Hispanic laity. Joe Caraballo had the clever idea of negotiating with the directors of these Bible schools (there are several dozen in the New York metropolitan area) for New York Theological Seminary, which had originally recruited their teachers, to provide them with continuing education. The result was the beginning of an Hispanic certificate program, also meeting on Saturdays at the seminary. It gradually attracted others; and while the English program usually numbered about one hundred, the Hispanic hovered at around fifty.

Thus by 1975–76 the programs that had been part of the vision of the seminary in 1970 had in many cases been altered or displaced, but an exciting new cluster of educational opportunities had emerged. People of faith could find an appropriate educational niche at New York Theological Seminary whatever their level of educational need—for those with less than a high school education there was the certificate program, for experienced mainline clergy the DMin, and many opportunities in between. It was with a real sense of gratitude that we recognized the extent to which we had been blessed by the leading of the Spirit; we still did not know where we would end up but were grateful for what had emerged.

While clergy of predominately white denominations continued in our STM and DMin programs, we were now dealing with large numbers of minority persons who dominated the certificate and college programs and were also a majority in the MDiv level courses. Note here also that another new constituency was emerging in our MDiv program. These were the second-career men and women, both white and black, who had long felt a calling to ministry, but had not had the opportunity to pursue this career. For women, this was usually the simple fact that until recently their churches did not ordain women. Many seminaries are finding their enrollments sustained by this constituency, but there was a different twist at NYTS. Our students were almost exclusively those for whom conventional scheduling and residential requirements made attendance impossible. I suspect that if other seminaries offered a full degree program in evening and weekend courses they would also find a ready student body.

Struggle and Conflict

Accredition. These years were not without struggle and conflict. The first complicating element was our relationship with the Association of Theological Schools. Clearly, the establishment was troubled by the developments in one of its accredited institutions. In retrospect we can be thankful for the sensitivity and genuine concern with which we were treated by the Commission on Accrediting. When in the spring of 1970 it became clear that we were going to terminate the faculty and launch out in a new direction, we wrote the ATS. In July we received this statement,

> The Commission heard the report of your progress with sympathy and wanted to provide a maximum period of time for NYTS to define its future program. Therefore, in the new listings of accredited schools, NYTS carries an asterisk with a note, "status under review, school undergoing process of redefining its program." After a thorough discussion, the group had determined that to place NYTS on probation would imply a quality of judgment that no one intended. Nor did it seem realistic to apply simply specific notations. I believe we all concluded that the above actions would alert interested parties to the changing of your institution and yet be eminently fair to your school.

That action gave us a breathing space while we undertook the restructuring of the seminary.

The next stage was a visit by a representative of the Committee on Accrediting, Herman Ritter, and by a staff member of the Association, David Schuller. It was clear that the seminary was still in a very difficult period of finding its future way. The result was a decision on the part of the Commission on Accrediting to allow us another eighteen months to complete the process of redefinition. It was clearly the best of all possible alternatives the commission might have taken at that point. We had a real sense of being provided moral support and space in which to find our own way without any negative judgment being made. But that was only the beginning. There were two major visits still to come. In December 1972 an evaluation team consisting of Joseph Deveney of Weston Seminary and Newell Wert of United Theological Seminary (Dayton) paid a formal visit to the seminary on behalf of the Commission on Accrediting. Their enthusiastic report was received with gratitude by all of us at NYTS. Their suggestions were very helpful. Their report included these words:

> Our general impression is that the administrative team is a group of able, innovating, and exciting educators who are not bound by institutional maintenance or tradition. They are clear about their goals and style and are above all desirous of assisting candidates to the fullest development of possession of their gifts of ministry. There is a high commitment to professional excellence, to personal growth, and to theological thinking in relation to life and practice. The administrators have an unusual degree of autonomy and freedom by virtue of the fact that they have no full-time faculty or students. They are able to pursue a kind of educational entrepreneurship not possible in more traditional institutions with an existing full-time community of learners both faculty and students.
>
> This is an interesting style, however difficult to evaluate. The likelihood that more of this kind of education eventually will develop suggests that the ATS give some thought to it especially in regard to: a) the school as broker of learning resources and the questions of the standards of control; b) the nature of internal checks and balances, provided for in other schools by a full-time faculty and student body; c) the means of pursuing a definitive and defining style of education using diverse people who may or may not understand or be competent in such a style. We find that the New York Theological Seminary appears at this stage to be functioning in a highly responsible way in all these areas.

With the receipt of that report we heaved a great sigh of relief. But when the report was considered by the Commission on Accrediting, they were not as confident as their accrediting team that the seminary met fully the standards of ATS. They placed several notations related to the adequacy of the library and the breadth of the faculty that had not been suggested by the team's report. We were safe, however, for another brief period of time.

Our request for the authorization of the DMin degree led to another accrediting visit on November 3–6, 1974. This was in effect our fourth significant encounter with the ATS in a little over four years. Once again, Dean Austin Deveney, a Jesuit priest, was chairperson of the team along with Dean Newell Wert. This time Professor Charles D. Gerkin of Candler School of Theology was added. From the point of view of NYTS it really was a great occasion.

It forced us to provide the committee with a very full self-study report. For the first time in four years the faculty and trustees received a very clear picture of the developing scope of our programs, an analysis of trends, job descriptions, and the financial situation. More importantly, the committee's visit once again produced a very strong affirmation of developments at the seminary. Its members probed very strenuously, met with groups of trustees, graduates, students, and faculty, and in the end wrote an even stronger report than two years earlier. This time they included as part of their general evaluation:

> The general impression is that NYTS, its administrative staff, adjunct faculty, and students are engaged in an experimental program of continuing education that is remarkably innovative and exciting. They are by and large clear about their goals and style and above all about their desire of assisting candidates to the fullest possible development of position of their use for ministry. This is particularly evident in the programmatic response to the peculiar needs of black, Hispanic, and other minority groups.
>
> Obviously an educational program that permits the situational problematic of contemporary society to set the agenda runs the risk of being judged as lacking in the historical and theological depth of core traditional curricular styles. Our clear impression is, however, that this risk is being taken with a high degree of awareness and responsibility. Both biblical and broadly theological concerns seem to have a central place in the various programs as that body of faith and tradition against which questions of contemporary life and professional practice must be pressed. Students are encouraged, even required, to "do theology."

With that report I was greatly relieved, suspecting that by the time the next visit would be due some ten years hence, there would be another president who would have to fill out all the forms and be responsible for the visit.

Relationship with Alumni. A second area that needed attention during these years was the relationship with the alumni. I mentioned earlier, the fierce loyalty of the older alumni to the institution which had made such an impact on their lives. But those who had continued to feel loyal to the seminary were by the time I arrived long disillusioned. Three presidents, one after another, had promised great new beginnings only to see the seminary seem ever more destined to collapse. At my first meeting with the alumni association at graduation in 1969 I had found a very mixed reception. There was obvious suspicion on the part of some, while several persons who had known me in the past were supportive and tried to be helpful in interpreting our situation to some of the others. One of the first things we did was to include three alumni elected by the alumni council as regular voting members of the board of trustees. I was pleased to have among those selected several who were loyal alumni but suspicious of the new president. That seemed the place to locate them—where they would have a chance to see the enthusiasm of the other trustees and know first-hand what was happening.

When the seminary went through the major transformation in the spring of 1970, the alumni council decided it was time to do a study of what was happening and to make recommendations that would help shape its developing life. A responsible group chaired by Samuel Blizzard of Princeton Seminary did this and made a full report in December 1971. On the whole the report recognized the need for significant changes in the seminary and that much of its program would have to be different from the patterns of the past. At the same time, the group was aware that the statutes of the seminary were very specific about the centrality of biblical study in the institution, including commitment to the inductive method, that the founder had made central. The report was rightly concerned that in the old days this had meant a biblically centered curriculum with half the courses involving study of one or more books of the Bible. No matter how committed we said we were to biblical study, the new programs, with the workshop pattern of the STM and the contextual curriculum of the MDiv level courses, did not have any place for such stress on specifically Bible content courses. I was genuinely convinced that in spirit we were fulfilling the mandate of the seminary and that our faculty was committed to a biblically centered faith, but that there was no way to shape a curriculum that would look like that of an earlier day.

In February the alumni study with its recommendations was presented to the faculty and trustees and led to what I felt was a very felicitous compromise. The trustees voted funds to hire a professor to fill the new Wilbert Webster White Chair of Biblical Studies. This person would be the one member of our core faculty team whose contract would provide for a significant amount of time for scholarly study. Once again, we were fortunate to discover Thomas Boomershine, then completing his PhD at Union, as an excellent choice for the chair. His work, which was in New Testament studies, highlighted the oral tradition through which much of scripture had been composed. His interests were about as close as one could hope to come to the emphases of the students of the inductive method. We arranged for him to be interviewed by alumni, including the last great proponent of the original form of inductive study, Robert Traina. His appointment was widely affirmed, to my great relief. Although there continued to be pockets of suspicion, by and large the alumni from that point forward became ever more supportive of the seminary including providing solid financial assistance.

Library. Another concern was for the library. With our program focused primarily on continuing and contextual education for MDiv level students, we had no need for a high percentage of the volumes in our library. However, the idea that we would actually sell part of the library struck horror in the hearts of the alumni and made the trustees very nervous. Our response was twofold. First, we talked to the librarians at Union and General to make sure that our faculty and students would have access to those superb facilities whenever that would be appropriate or helpful. Secondly, we arranged for a group of consultant scholars to look at our curriculum and our plans for the next two years and then to pull off the shelves every book they thought any students would use now or in the immediate future. We sold the remaining 35,000 volumes to the highest bidder for $111,000, leaving us with about 10,000 books. The library was then able to fit comfortably into approximately one-quarter of the space that it had previously occupied. We were able to rent the other three-quarters to compatible organizations for approximately $30,000 a year. As can be imagined, the sale of our library did raise questions on the two accrediting visits in 1972 and 1974, but we were able to demonstrate that our students had access to a variety of libraries in the New York metropolitan area, that in most cases they purchased the books required for their courses, and that they did in fact make extensive use of our own library and those at General and Union Theological seminaries.

Seminary Property. A fourth area of concern during this period had to do with the seminary property. On either side of the main building on 49th Street were residential properties. One was an apartment building with four very attractive apartments, one on each floor; on the other side was a brownstone with three apartments. The decision had been made in 1970 to sell these properties in order to find funds for faculty termination payments. While they were desirable properties in relatively good shape, we had considerable difficulty in disposing of them for a price which ten years later seemed pathetically small, but which at the time was fully satisfactory. The net sale came to approximately $235,000. This enabled us to repay the several loans which had enabled us to survive through 1969–70 and made the faculty termination payments of about $100,000.

The final property issue came over the future of our main building. This large facility, with a gymnasium in the basement, five residential floors, classrooms, library, chapel, and refectory had been a great asset during the years when the seminary was a very tightly knit residential community. But now we were using only four of the twelve floors. Two issues emerged rather quickly. First, there was a serious maintenance problem. It seemed that every time we turned around there was a leak in the roof or a break in the plumbing or the elevators were out of order. We clearly had a deteriorating facility that would take very considerable funds to maintain. Shortly after I arrived at the seminary, I discovered that a college classmate, head of one of the major real estate consulting firms in the city, was the consultant to St. Peter's Church on its property developments. As a favor to us, he took a look at our situation and strongly recommended that we consider selling the property and moving to more appropriate facilities. This seemed like very extreme action, but beginning in 1971 the trustees did take this under advisement and indicated that they would be open to an appropriate offer in the neighborhood of $3,000,000. The crunch came when the mayor of New York decided there was too much tax-exempt property in the city and sent tax assessors to place back on the tax roles as much exempt property as possible, thus requiring the owners to justify their exemption. The seminary received a tax bill in 1975 that forced us into a court hearing and a drawn out legal struggle with the tax commission. This underlined the advisability of getting out from under the property altogether. At that time the real estate market was quite depressed and we finally accepted an offer of approximately $1,000,000 in late spring, 1976. The tax commission determined that approximately twenty-five percent of the building was used for non-tax-exempt purposes, and we paid a relatively modest amount in back taxes before we could complete the sale.

Faculty Morale. Another element of concern during this period was development of faculty morale. During 1970–71 the core group consisted of only five persons, each responsible for one of the three circles plus the president and an administrative associate. Gradually however, others were added, making a core team of eight persons called the administrative faculty. Our piecework salary pattern looked like this. Each sector of our work had a price tag. The dean of a program might receive $5,000 for that work; each course might produce $2,000 dollars of income, and so on. The assumption was that members of the administrative core would have their primary base at the seminary, giving it priority in their overall ministry. At the same time, each of us would have a modest involvement in some ministry in the metropolitan area. One person might function as an assistant pastor in a congregation, working there on weekends, another as part-time staff in an social action program or as the chairperson of the board of a community corporation.

Our problem was to develop a sense of ownership and collegiality in what we were about. The sense of commitment emerged through a cluster of developments. We began to meet weekly for an hour-and-a-half, focusing on regular Bible study as a symbol of our commitment to a biblical faith and as a way of implementing the centrality of the Word in our life. These were not primarily academic, but a corporate effort to explore the meaning of a passage for our personal lives and for the work of the seminary—harking back to my East Harlem Parish days. When the accrediting team from the AATS was holding its exit visit with the faculty, they told us that we were "a confessional seminary." Not sure at first if this was to be taken positively, we discovered that it was very affirming and something unique in the experience of the team. They were referring to the fact that in spite of our wide differences—denominational, theological, ethnic, and sexual—we did have a common commitment to biblical faith and gathered weekly around the study of the scriptures. That to them was a rather unexpected discovery in a seminary. And while not designed as a public relations ploy, our weekly Bible study did help disarm a lot of skeptical alumni!

A second factor that held us together was the commitment to spend June of each year in a very strenuous evaluation of each of our previous year's programs, in careful planning for the following year, and in a week of continuing education that we did as a group followed by a three-day retreat outside the city. This became significant in building a sense of mutual trust and accountability. One year, a week was spent in an immersion into the black and Hispanic urban communities of New York City. Another year the faculty lived at the Interdenominational Theological Seminary in Atlanta, Georgia. While exploring the dynamics of the black community in Atlanta, we also attended a meeting of the Society for Continuing Education in Ministry. Another summer we spent a week together in Puerto Rico exploring the life and problems of that community from which so many of our students came. Finally, we were knit together by the commitment to ongoing evaluation and mutual feedback. Several times during the year, the faculty would meet all day to check up on our morale and to provide each other with feedback on our academic performance and administrative functioning, trying in every possible way to help all of us to focus our energy on those things we did well and to enhance our own competence. By 1975, the faculty included black, Hispanic, and women members, as well as the original male Caucasians.[2]

Board of Trustees. A final area for attention during this five-year period was the board of trustees. During its entire previous history, the president of the seminary had been chairperson of the executive committee of the trustees and had exercised strong control. Furthermore, historically the trustees had exercised their authority in sharp isolation from the faculty and students. Old minutes indicate that during the trying years of the great depression, the faculty had pleaded with the trustees for time on the agenda of a regular meeting only to be rejected. The style of trustee operation reflected very much a strong tradition of paternalism. Now it was in order to seek a more collegial pattern with a sense of partnership in a common task. It was also apparent that the most urgent requirement was for trustees who would reflect the ethnic and racial diversity at New York Theological Seminary. We were fortunate in securing men and women who were deeply respected in the black and Hispanic as well as mainline white religious communities in New York City. The trustees functioned collegially rather than authoritatively. Trustees were regularly involved with faculty in program planning and evaluation, were encouraged to participate in search committees for new faculty members, and in general were looked upon as partners in the seminary program. In return, faculty regularly attended trustee meetings, and, although without vote, participated actively in the discussions.

A key pattern for securing involvement was the program committee structure. This was modeled after the visiting committees through which alumni participate in the life of Harvard

2. For a full discussion of faculty patterns and functioning, see Monograph IV: *The Administrative Faculty: The Search for Collegiality.*

University. Each major program area had its own committee chaired by a member of the board of trustees and made up of three or four additional trustees as well as representatives of the alumni and student body. This committee served as a support and consulting group for the dean of the program but, more importantly, provided a regular means for trustees to understand in some depth at least one of the many varied program elements of the seminary. The program committees were available for advice and support, but also were responsible for seeing that a careful evaluation program was established and carried out. They also served as interpreters of the program to the full board of trustees.[3]

The program committee pattern was supplemented by the development of a program budget process for our finances. Harold Midtbo had seen the usefulness of this method of accounting in the work of the national boards of the American Lutheran Church and this was an excellent pattern for NYTS. It enabled us to discover and monitor quite clearly the actual costs for each of our eight to ten major program components. The budget for each program was kept on one page, with income which would be generated from tuition and fees as well as from any restricted foundation grants listed on the top half. The specific costs for each of the educational components of that one program were recorded on the bottom half. We were able to calculate these figures because we paid our staff on the piecework pattern. We could determine precisely what subsidy would be necessary to cover the difference between educational expenses and assured income. Finally, the overhead costs of the seminary not directly attributable to any one program were totaled and then divided in an appropriate pattern among the program budgets. In this way we could determine the real costs of each of our different operations and assess each value in relationship to cost.

These program budgets were not only an excellent means for cost accounting and evaluation but were also very effective in seeking foundation support. It was apparent that the founda-

---

3. For a full discussion of the trustee pattern, see Monograph VI: *The Trustee Pattern*.

tion grantors were impressed by our good control over our finances and delighted to know that a grant made for a specific purpose would in fact be utilized for that very focused undertaking and would not get lost in the overall budgets.[4]

The relationship between faculty and trustees was marred by only one heavy encounter. After several years of our new style, some of the administrative faculty and a few of the trustees began to worry about the matter of continuity and security of faculty who received appointments for only one year at a time. This produced a rather unprepared suggestion from the president that we consider returning to a normal pattern of full-time faculty and even the possibility of longer appointments. A number of the trustees reacted to this heresy with horror. Their reaction led in 1974 to a fresh look at our pattern which produced a decision to reject the tenure pattern, to encourage faculty to continue with a limited involvement in ministry outside the seminary, but to provide appointments for two-year periods with an evaluation six months before the time for renewal. Faculty/trustee relationships were strengthened by an annual retreat each January at some location away from the seminary. These were not occasions for business but for deepening friendships, for Bible study and worship, and for a look at overall policy issues discussion.

---

4. For a discussion of seminary fund-raising, see Monograph V: *Finances of New York Theological Seminary.*

CHAPTER 3

Stability and Change

1975–1979

It was now unambiguously clear that the future of the seminary was directly linked to the life of New York City and the metropolitan area. In 1975 the city was in the depths of a financial crisis, the result of a cluster of factors that brought it to the brink of bankruptcy. For our constituency, now predominantly black and Hispanic, it underlined what many knew so well: the war on poverty, with all its promises for a better future for those on the lower end of the economic scale, had proved to be less than successful. This recognition, coupled with the new sense of identity that was a positive legacy of the civil rights movement of the sixties, produced a new awareness in our students of the need for sociological and political analysis. There was a new openness to discover the biblical mandate to work for the improvement of the community and to undertake programs in social welfare and social action.

Another legacy of the previous ten years was from the women's movement. Among our white female students there was a clear imperative to deal with issues of sexism in the church and society as well as in the patterns of seminary life and teaching. Although feminist thinking had not penetrated very far in many of the black and Hispanic congregations, many women from these communities were coming to the seminary eager to prepare for ordination and to fight for their place in the leadership of the churches.

By the beginning of the 1975–76 academic year the seminary had reached a certain level of stability. Our basic programs in the three circles were now in place and the faculty had been significantly strengthened by the addition of Diana Beach to work with Mel Schoonover as the assistant in our degree programs and provide a significant female presence. She was a graduate of Berkeley Divinity School and was shortly to be ordained an Episcopal priest. She brought impressive counseling skills as well as a strong feminist perspective to the administrative faculty. At the same time, Doria Donnelly, a Roman Catholic theologian who had been teaching at Fordham University, became the administrator of our programs for laity. She was the first Roman Catholic to serve the seminary on a regular basis.

These years from 1975–79 were also marked by adequate financing through our combination of tuition, modest endowment, annual giving, and continued strong foundation grants. Thus I found myself spending no more than ten percent of my time in fund-raising. With unambiguous trustee support for undertaking new ventures, priority could be given to responding to a wide range of educational needs in our diverse constituency.

Throughout these years, there was never any great difficulty in taking on a new program as long as we had the necessary personnel resources and funds. The trustees did worry about size. There was a clear stipulation that no major new program would be undertaken until an existing one was phased out. We held to this very consistently, but there were occasions when a new program was slipped in as an aspect of one of our current areas of work. In considerable measure, we were able to live up to our image as a pilgrim seminary with the flexibility, resources, and energy to be open to these new challenges.

The Seventy-Fifth Anniversary

The fall of 1975 marked a major turning point in our relationship with the alumni and the development of a far stronger sense of continuity with the earlier decades of the Biblical Seminary. Ever since the name had been changed in 1965, seminary stationary and literature had always added the phrase, "continuing the Biblical Seminary in New York." For many alumni, this statement was a little dubious if not downright misleading. When I first came to the seminary, in reading the biography of Dr. White I had come to a personal conclusion that our spirit resonated with his and that much of what we did might have been affirmed by our founder. Many alumni doubted this. The seventy-fifth anniversary gave us a wonderful opportunity to bring back to the seminary for a weekend over a hundred and fifty alumni who had studied at the seminary between 1920 and 1950. They came in part because the last great Biblical Seminary president, Dean G. McKee, agreed to be present as a speaker along with another distinguished alumna, Professor Rachel Henderlite from Austin Theological Seminary, a Presbyterian seminary in Austin, Texas. The alumni board was also able to convince people from the earlier years that a number of their classmates would be present and that whatever their attitude toward the present administration of the seminary, they would have a wonderful reunion. I thoroughly enjoyed the weekend myself in spite of strong misgivings in the weeks before.

The mechanics of the event, beginning on Saturday at noon and ending on Sunday night, readily fell into place. The facilities at a major downtown hotel were satisfactory. The workshops were very effective, the Bible study groups were great, and we had an outstanding opening address by a well-known black evangelist, Tom Skinner. His strong affirmation of the present programs of the seminary set a good tone. More importantly, he spoke powerfully about the gospel mandate to meet human needs in the city and to work for justice in society.

The workshops were led by current faculty and gave the alumni a good opportunity to catch something of the ethos of current seminary teaching and emphases. There was also a healthy mix of recent graduates who had previously known nothing about the traditions of Biblical Seminary. The mix worked very well.

The celebration exceeded our hopes. In a major address on Sunday evening, former president Dean McKee, while reminiscing about the past, gave very strong support to present development at the seminary. He said in part, "What the Biblical Seminary set out to be is needed now as much or more than ever before. When I read that the present faculty engage in prayer and Bible study I recognized in the New York Theological Seminary of today the continuation of the Biblical Seminary in New York of yesterday. I rejoice in what is being done here today, improving on what we tried to do back then." Concluding he said, "We sometimes viewed life in this seminary as 'God at work in the life of an institution,' and I've been hearing from some of our present students that this is still true."

In my own presentation I hit on the image of a marriage and suggested that the traditions of Biblical Seminary had been married to the experience and background of an urban ministry commitment to create the new institution. One side of the family was emphasized in the speech by Dean McKee and included the following elements:

1. The Bible at the center of training of Christian leadership;
2. Wide representation of Protestant denominations;
3. High standards of scholarship;
4. Engaged in and tested by practical outreach;
5. Emphasis upon prayer, worship and community.

From the other side have come such contributions as:

1. An abiding concern for the New York metropolitan area and expertise in meeting its challenge as Christians;
2. Commitment to continuing education for clergy as today's urgent priority;
3. Experience in opening educational doors for black and Hispanic clergy, often excluded from higher education;
4. A capacity for experimentation, including risk taking, flexibility, and willingness to submit to regular evaluation;
5. A vision of the seminary as a resource for the full Christian community in its task of mission and ministry.

The point of the metaphor was to stress that the present programs of the seminary, the offspring of these two family lines, ought to bear a strong family resemblance to both, and yet be a genuinely new creation. I came away from the celebration weekend with new assurance that the older alumni now believed that our present style and program was a legitimate heir of Biblical Seminary and were prepared to support us with prayer, interest, and money. They had recognized that New York Theological Seminary was maintaining the traditional commitment to a solid grounding in the scriptures, creation of a strong sense of community among faculty and students, and a concern for the city.

Shortly after this October gathering an issue of the seminary bulletin with a collection of pictures and reports on those present was mailed out. It persuaded many of those not present that New York Theological Seminary was indeed continuing the Biblical Seminary in New York. In subsequent visits in various parts of the country, I encountered alumni at meetings who expressed their satisfaction with what was happening at "Biblical" and their delight that their alma mater was alive and well, after so many reports of either its death or unfortunate deviation from the past.

Several years later this conviction was reinforced by the report of the Auburn study on the history of theological education. In the course of this study, a young researcher, Virginia Brereton, examined the emergence of Bible schools and colleges during the early part of the twentieth century. In the course of this she took a hard look at Biblical Seminary. In company with the director of the project, Robert Lynn, Brereton spent several sessions with faculty and trustees sharing the results of the study. It became quite clear that to a degree far beyond what we had suspected, there was a true sense of continuity in spirit and in style between the early Biblical Seminary and what was happening currently at New York Theological Seminary. This was evidenced at least by these points:

1. Centrality of the Bible (in English): the study of the scriptures in a disciplined way as a critical element in the whole life of the institution;
2. Emphasis on practical experience;
3. Clear recognition that it was a professional school with every right to emphasize training in the skills required for ministry;
4. Accessibility to a wide range of students and denominations;
5. Responsiveness to the city and involvement in its life;
6. Prominence of women in the faculty and the presence of women in the student body in significant numbers;
7. A large lay training role with genuine commitment to providing educational opportunities for lay persons in the metropolitan area churches;
8. A commitment to academic excellence;
9. A concern for ethnic ministry through the development of an Italian department in the earlier years and a commitment to Hispanic work at the present;
10. The development of an extension department beginning in 1910;
11. Beginning in 1921 Biblical Seminary had a major component under the heading of "Continuing Edu-

cation for Pastors" that is a central focus of the seminary today;

12. A determination then and now that the faculty would not simply be scholar-teachers but would also be deeply involved in the life of the churches in the metropolitan area.

All this was very reassuring in terms of our integrity and of our relationship to the alumni. The one really sticky point involved the statutes of the seminary. From the very beginning Dr. White had apparently been concerned not only that biblical studies be the central core of the seminary's life and curriculum, but also that this particular method of inductive Bible study be seen as absolutely essential to the institution. Thus while the statutes as a whole required faculty, trustees, and students to affirm their commitment to biblical studies and to this particular method of acquiring biblical knowledge, the requirement could be changed by a vote of four-fifths of all living trustees present and voting. Any trustee who questioned this provision, however, was expected to resign! This made it virtually impossible to change this traditional wording. But our own integrity seemed to demand that we find a legitimate way to bring the statutes into conformity with the new shape of the seminary. There was simply no logic in forcing a particular method into our new programs.

Gradually, with the help of our attorneys, a strategy for revision was designed and implemented. The total document was redrafted using, wherever possible, the language and emphasis of the original. Much of what was in Section 12, the sticky point, was simply taken over as the preface, with the elimination of the demand for a particular biblical method. It was discussed by the trustees at several meetings, sent out to a large number of respected older alumni for their suggestions with an explanation of our concern, then modestly revised. The new statutes were under consideration for two more years while we more or less operated under their provisions but made no attempt to pass them. They were then brought out again, revised in several minor ways in light of our experience with them and once again distributed to trustees, faculty, and alumni for any further thoughts. By this time everybody was tired of the whole process. Any residual opposition had evaporated. Now the administration and the trustees could feel that the statutes reflected the life of the seminary and were at the same time genuinely faithful to the spirit of the Biblical Seminary.

The Move from Forty-Ninth Street

The second major event during this half decade was the sale of the property on 49th Street and the move to new facilities on 29th Street just off Fifth Avenue. Thoughts of selling the building had been entertained almost from the beginning of my time at NYTS. With the dramatic change in 1970 from a residential student body to an entirely commuting one, we no longer had use for most of the space. But it was also clear that a number of other elements went into the rationale for the sale. First was the steady deterioration of the property, which placed a constant drain on our income. Second, the demands of building care and, in particular, the needs of the residential tenants were a considerable administrative diversion from the work of the seminary. We were in effect running a hotel whose occupants required an unbelievable range of attention and care. In the third place, we were facing the tax problems noted earlier. In other words, the building was a fading financial asset. We watched the net income steadily dwindle as expenses, particularly utilities, dramatically increased. If we did not get out of ownership, we would again be in the position of being property poor.

When in August 1976, we finally received a concrete and reasonable offer of 1.1 million dollars, we accepted quickly. Some months before, I had slipped into a bottom drawer a real estate announcement that several floors were for rent in property owned by the Collegiate Corporation at 5 West 29th Street. The day we signed the purchase agreement I pulled the flier out of the drawer and called the agent to see if the space was still available. He indicated that three floors were still on the market and that he would be glad to show them to me. That same day three of us from the seminary had a look at the space in a ten-story office building adjacent to and partly used by Marble

Collegiate Church. It had been badly used by the previous occupants and would require a good deal of remodeling, but it seemed to have many advantages. Nevertheless, we hired two young seminary graduates with a dual assignment: (1) to scour the midtown area for the most acceptable possible location for us within reasonable distance from major transportation arteries, Grand Central Terminal, and Penn Station, and (2) to relocate all our tenants with as much assistance and as little pain as possible. When the search was over we were convinced that the space on 29th Street was by far the most advantageous available and in the fall signed a lease with the Collegiate Corporation. It provided for our taking over initially two full floors with the understanding that we would have access to space used by the church when our needs and their availability coincided.

A real crisis arose when, about the time we signed the lease on the property and on the last day before the option to purchase our old building ran out, the prospective buyer withdrew. After helpful advice from our real estate consultant and trustee John White, we voted to sign the lease and move when the space would be ready in January, even if our present facilities had not been sold. Very anxious and hectic months ensued, but in early December another contract to sell was signed, this time for $1,000,000. Permission to sell such an asset had to be obtained from the State Education department and the courts, but in due time this was received and two months later an empty building was turned over to the new landlords.

We were fortunate in securing alternative housing for those in our building who were dependent on us for help in making the transition. We had no lawsuits, nor did we create any strong hostility among those who were displaced.

On February 6, 1977 after some weeks of delay, we celebrated our relocation by a march through the city streets from the old building to the new location and by a service of worship in the sanctuary of Marble Collegiate Church. It was a blustery cold day on which we marched with a police escort across 49th Street to Lexington Avenue, down Lexington Avenue to 29th Street and over three blocks to the new location. We certainly felt like the pilgrim people we claimed to be.

Our expectations proved justified. The location was superb not only because of its accessibility to public transportation but also because the streets in that area are available for parking after 6:00 P.M. on weekdays and all day Saturday, the times when the great majority of our classes were held. Eventually, it was necessary to take over the seventh floor to provide facilities for the branch campus of the College of New Rochelle. Relations with the church have always been harmonious. They now use our classroom space for their Sunday school and in return make available to us their large meeting rooms, catering service, sanctuary, and chapel. In a neighborhood where commercial property rented by non-profit organizations often comes to seventeen or eighteen dollars a square foot, our cost as worked out through the shared expense pattern by the Collegiate Corporation was about four dollars a square foot. Thus the income from the investment of the proceeds of the sale of the old building covered our total cost for facilities with nearly fifty percent of the proceeds left over for our general operating expenses. In the fall of 1982 I asked the president of Union Theological Seminary what their utility bill was for a year. It was then in the neighborhood of $400,000, whereas our total cost for property including utilities was about $50,000. Of course the institutions are in no way comparable, but the figures do reflect the fact that the cost effectiveness of NYTS had been a very important element in our viability.

Academic Programs[1]

During the period from 1975 to 1979, the basic structures of our academic work continued to be best described by the three-circle model. The *certificate program* continued to develop as an all-day-Saturday program offered in both English and Spanish for twenty-eight weeks during the academic year.

The second circle was the *college program*. Our frustration over the expense of our arrangement with Adelphi University

1. For a fuller discussion of our curricular patterns, see Monograph I: *Pedagogy: The Scope and Rationale of the Various Programs.*

and the great difficulty experienced by Empire State College, with its very limited resources, in handling our large group of students led us to discover (with great relief) the College of New Rochelle. Negotiations began there in the summer of 1977. They assigned a very able Roman Catholic sister, Eleanor Shea, to act as director of the seminary extension program. By the end of 1977 it was quite clear that the potential enrollment was far greater than we had anticipated, which led the college first to rent the entire seventh floor from us and then to seek permission to make their work on 29th Street a branch campus. When this permission was granted, students could take their entire academic program at 29th Street, whereas in an extension program they would have been required to do some work at the main campus. New York Theological Seminary was responsible for recruiting men and women who could profit from this particular pattern and who could also assist in advising and teaching. I had thought that 200 students would be as many as we could hope to recruit and that the college could handle effectively. Eventually, we watched the numbers move steadily from sixty-five to seventy the first year to a normal registration of approximately 300.

The college program meets a tremendous need among minority men and women who come out of a strong religious background. The courses are held primarily in the evening, which makes them readily available. Considerable credit is given for relevant life experience and for bilingual competence, but above all the teachers recognize that the students are mature men and women with proof of leadership competence in their own communities and deserve to be treated more as colleagues than as pupils. The college has also been flexible in developing curricular elements beyond the basic core requirements to meet the particular needs of these students. Thus during several weeks in the fall, courses could be proposed by students, seminary, or the college staff itself. As many as fifty options would be listed each on a sheet of paper posted on the wall of the student lounge. If over fifteen students indicated their willingness to undertake that particular course, an appropriate instructor would be found and the course would be offered during the next semester. This gave the students a real sense of participation and ownership in the program itself. Now sixty to seventy-five students a year are completing the requirements for a fully accredited bachelor of arts degree.

The third circle, *seminary degree programs,* was the most varied and complex as the seminary sought to respond to a wide range of student constituencies under the basic headings of the DMin, STM, and MDiv degrees. The DMin program is a good illustration. Beginning in the fall of 1974, the doctor of ministry program quickly became an important program element. The original design was for men and women functioning as clergy in a parish setting. In comparison with the wide range of such degrees being developed in Protestant seminaries across the country, this gave strong emphasis to the development of competence in the particular work of ministry in which the candidate was presently engaged. While this required demonstrated ability to reflect theologically on ministry, it gave priority to the enhancement of professional skills and understanding. One distinctive ingredient was the requirement that the student develop a "site team," a group of representative lay persons who would provide honest feedback on performance, work with the candidate on defining goals, and work with the seminary in assessment. When an effective site team emerged, it became a superb resource for the clergyperson and demonstrated the value of lay leadership and teamwork in the parish. However, located as we are in New York City, we are surrounded by men and women who function as executives in various denominational bureaucracies. Thus the second focus of our DMin was for church bureaucrats who wanted to develop the competencies required for administrative positions. Rather than meeting for one day a week during the first year of the program, the executive DMin group would meet two days, usually including an overnight once a month, for a full two-year period. This was much more practical, given their travel commitments and other responsibilities. T. Richard Snyder, appointed dean of the doctoral programs beginning in 1978, proved to be highly skilled in working with this group.

Several extension DMins were begun in response to cries

for help.[2] A number of men in Maine who had been involved in our STM program begged us to offer them a DMin degree since nothing was available closer than Boston. In 1977, we selected eight of the outstanding graduates and located a very able teaching team to provide the first year of instruction. Jim Claque, who had retired as a professor of theology at Berkeley Divinity School at Yale, and his wife, Susan Claque-Davis, who had several years earlier been awarded a DMin degree from New York Theological Seminary, were living in Maine. They provided the basic supervision of the first year. Staff from the seminary, first Mel Schoonover and then myself, worked with the site teams and took responsibility for the demonstration project work, thus providing first-hand input from the seminary faculty.

The second extension DMin program was organized in Washington, D.C. A dozen black clergy, mostly Methodist, learned of our DMin pattern, and after several trips to New York to investigate, asked that we consider offering it in the Washington, D.C. area. This was a little embarrassing. They had all attended one of the first-rate seminaries in the area but did not find the DMin programs offered there as relevant to their needs as what they found at New York Theological Seminary. From their perspective what they needed was a DMin program that clearly was designed to focus on parish ministry. They were also attracted by our insistence that they develop a group of laity who would join with them in the whole process. It was finally agreed that we could provide as mentor in the D.C. area, William Hayes, who had served on the staff of INTER-MET. They would meet in Washington for three all-day sessions each month. The fourth week they would travel to New York for a full eight hours of work with our faculty. That made for a fairly exhausting schedule, but the basic shape of the program followed our own patterns of providing on-the-job training.

The third DMin program to emerge, and one which continued to raise questions with the accrediting body, is in Sheffield, England. During my first full year at New York Theo-

---

2. For a full discussion of dispersed programs, see Monograph VII: *Cooperative and Dispersed Programs.*

logical Seminary, John Vincent had been visiting professor in the spring semester. He had visited the seminary regularly in subsequent years while functioning as head of what is called the Urban Training Unit in Sheffield. He is a rare combination of scholar and church person whose passion has been to equip men and women in England for urban ministry. Since nothing like a DMin degree was offered in England, he badgered us for several years to permit him to offer a degree for qualified British clergy. It was finally worked out, with Vincent serving as the basic mentor, with the entire group coming to New York Theological Seminary for two weeks twice during their time in the program and our dean visiting Sheffield for several days twice each year. As with our other degree programs, the rule of thumb was that the direct cost of the program should be covered by tuition generated. But it remained difficult to demonstrate that NYTS did indeed play a sufficient role in supervising the program or could justify the logic of undertaking work in such a different context and at such a distance.

Another area of substantial enrollment was in our work in *pastoral counseling*. For the period 1968–75 the enrollment of forty to fifty students a year at the Post-Graduate Center for Mental Health had been our bread and butter. Nearly all the students in its two-year program registered for our STM degree, taking one course at the seminary each semester during their four-semester enrollment. However, with the rapid development around the country of DMin programs, enrollment at the STM degree level began to drop off rather sharply. While some students continued to register at the Post-Graduate Center and for clinical pastoral education work at several New York City hospitals, several similar dispersed programs came into the picture. The first was an excellent pastoral counseling program and clergy training center connected with Trinity Church in Princeton, New Jersey, a block from Princeton Theological Seminary. They provided training for clergy in the New Jersey area and were eager to offer it for credit following somewhat the pattern of our relationship with the Post-Graduate Center for Mental Health. We urged them to work with Princeton Seminary, which had an excellent pastoral counseling department and was readily available. However, Trinity was unable to find any support at Princeton for such a relationship, I gather largely on the grounds that the program was far too professional and not sufficiently academic to seem appropriate to the Princeton faculty or administration. They thus turned again to us. Since the basic focus of the program was in New Jersey, we had to seek permission from the State Education Department to offer this degree. We had not been through such a process before and were uncertain how it would work out. We discovered that the state questioned other seminaries in the area as to whether the program was something that they wanted to do and whether it would be unfair competition. We gathered that Princeton University objected: but as it was not willing to undertake such a program, the State Education Department had the feeling that its disapproval did not carry sufficient weight. Thus after a hearing with the State Education Department, permission was granted us to offer the STM degree. Approximately two-thirds of the work was undertaken at the Trinity Counseling Center, with our own faculty offering the remainder either at Princeton Seminary or through a course at NYTS.

The final pastoral counseling option came through a program developed by Wainwright House in Rye, New York. This well-known lay retreat center had begun a program to train spiritual guides and wanted to offer credit where this would be appropriate. This program, called The Guild For Spiritual Guidance, was investigated at some length by Diana Beach, then the dean of our pastoral counseling program, who herself enrolled in the first two-year program along with another of our contract faculty. Students could apply their work at the Guild as one-half of the thirty-six credits required for the master of professional studies (MPS) degree from New York Theological Seminary.

In every case, these diverse programs resulted from no long-range planning on our part, but were developed in response to clearly articulated needs of students that demanded help from NYTS. The commitment of the faculty, and in particular the deans, to take on this additional work grew, I think, out of a genuine concern to insure that men and women committed to Christian ministry in its various forms were given appropriate academic credit for work which would more fully equip them for the task to which they were called.

To clarify our curriculum situation during 1978–79, let me conclude with a summary of our programs and a brief word about each.[3]

Program Summary 1978–79

I. Non-Degree Programs

A. *Certificate programs for church leaders (clergy and lay):* These are held on Saturdays at the seminary, one program in English and one in Spanish. They provide basic courses for those engaged in urban ministry: preaching workshops, biblical studies, urban analysis and the like. At the conclusion of 28 weeks a certificate is awarded in urban ministry.

Enrollment:	Fall 1978	Spring 1979
English	98	120
Spanish	42	65

B. *Mid-Life Exploration:* A year-long seminar, meeting every other week for five hours. For men and women who wish to engage in serious study and reflection on their faith and life. Can be taken for credit.

Enrollment:	12	12
	152	197

II. College Program for Clergy

An accredited bachelor's program offered by the College of New Rochelle, with courses held at the seminary. Designed for church members, with provisions for life experience credit and advanced standing for previous academic work even in Bible

3. Cf. Monograph III: *Particular Seminary Programs.*

schools. Courses provide a broad liberal arts education, but with the present vocational needs of urban Christians in mind.

Enrollment:

College of New Rochelle	168	196
Other colleges	31	32
	199	228

III. Seminary Degree Programs

A. *Master's in Parish Ministry or Pastoral Counseling:* Degree awarded is STM (for those with MDiv) or MPS (for those with AB). Requires one day per week for two years. On-the-job training, in context of peer education, designed to improve competence in the work of ministry.

Enrollment:	59	55

B. *Doctor of Ministry:* The emphasis is upon demonstrating a high level of competence and maturity in the ministry of the candidate. One important requirement involves creation of a team of lay colleagues who share in the educational process.

Enrollment:	54	53

C. *Master of Divinity:* For mature church leaders who now seek ordination and for those who are unable to attend a regular residential seminary. Requires two evenings per week for four years, plus two intensive weeks at New Brunswick Theological Seminary each of three summers.

Enrollment:	37	37

D. *Master of Professional Studies in Christian Education:* Designed for church leaders in Christian educational programs including church school superintendents, teachers, and youth leaders, and conducted in cooperation with New York University.

Enrollment:	5	5

E. *Unclassified students taking various courses.*

Enrollment:	8	6
	163	156
Total enrollment:	514	581

The master of divinity program requires a special word. It developed dramatically during this period as we worked jointly with New Brunswick Theological Seminary. It was given the title "Joint MPS/MDiv Degree" since it was designed to admit students first for the master of professional studies degree with the expectation of professional competence, followed by the master of divinity degree with its heavy academic expectations. During the first year of study, students took a workshop in the practice of parish ministry and a specifically academic course in introduction to theology or biblical studies. If during that year they proved able to handle the demands of the MDiv, they were allowed to transfer to New Brunswick and continue toward the MDiv degree. If, however, their time constraints or other factors made it impossible for them to give the time and energy required for the four-year MDiv degree, they continued in our parish ministry workshops to the thirty-six credit professional degree in the practice of parish ministry.

By 1977 we had completed the fourth year of this unique degree program. It provided access to theological degree credentials to a wide range of church leaders who heretofore had been locked out of the system. We were genuinely startled to discover, as the program developed, that we had tapped into a deep reservoir of persons who had long felt a calling to ordained ministry, but for a variety of reasons had not been able to respond. A black high school principal, working as a lay leader, found far more satisfaction in his church work. A state prison guard had returned to college to prepare for a second career in ministry and then discovered that his bishop required a seminary degree. A young black woman who was employed as a copy editor, having always felt called to ordination, suddenly discovered that her local Baptist church had called a pastor who was willing to support her in fulfilling her call, a possibility heretofore totally denied.

For all of these people and many more, NYTS provided the resource they had to have. There was no other program anywhere that did not require full-time or at least day-time attendance. It was possible for mature men and women with substantial job and family responsibilities to find a path to an MDiv degree, albeit a long and difficult one. For the faculty, the students provided a unique experience for two reasons: unlike many who came to seminary (in those days), they were mature in their faith and unambiguously committed to the vocation of ordained ministry; at the same time they were already rooted in a situation of ministerial responsibility and were clearly marked as church leaders. As a result the faculty found that the usual problems of motivation and relevance were nonexistent and that they could get on with the central task in any given course.[4]

The students themselves continue to fall into very interesting groups. Roughly one third of the eighty or so who had begun the program by 1978 were mature and experienced clergy, both black and Hispanic, who wanted the legitimacy and credential of the MDiv degree, although it did not necessarily have any significance in their career pattern. Another third were church leaders in their thirties and forties who decided to seek ordination and were members of denominations that required the MDiv degree. They were teachers, social workers, police officers, and a growing number of women seeking a second vocation. Many in this group were white. The final third were young Hispanic and black church leaders, both ordained and lay, who wanted to retain their present leadership roles in their own religious communities and so did not wish to pack off to a traditional seminary for three years. The full MDiv degree could be completed at NYTS in four years through attendance at classes in New York for two evenings each week during the academic year plus two weeks in residence at New Brunswick in each of two summers. It was a terribly heavy schedule. At the end of the first four years, five students out of an initial group of seventeen had actually completed the program.

---

4. For a fuller discussion of our constituency, see Monograph II: *The Constituency of New York Theological Seminary.*

We have discovered that nearly all of the men and women who enrolled had the intelligence, preparation, and confidence to complete an MDiv degree, but nearly half were unable to carve out from already heavy schedules the study time to meet the requirements of their courses. Those who did make it gave promise of a high level of leadership in the years ahead.

During these years several nagging concerns were always coming to the surface. One was the desire on the part of all faculty and trustees to remain as inclusive and diverse as possible in our work. As the college and certificate programs grew dramatically, there was some fear that we might lose our white constituents altogether. They tended to cluster in our degree programs, but we worked hard to encourage them to enroll in the certificate program and in the second career exploration. Our inclusiveness was also helped by the fact that beginning in 1975 there were always at least two women members of the administrative faculty and, beginning in 1978, several Hispanics and blacks out of a total of ten. The trustees also reflected this diversity of black, Hispanic, and white lay and clergy throughout the period.

The second concern was our responsibility for women in ministry and also for the serious problems of sexism faced by women in all the churches of this city including many of the black and Hispanic congregations. Doris Donnelly and Diana Beach, while hired for specific administrative responsibilities, were also strongly encouraged to respond to any needs that might emerge among women interested in preparing for ordination. What did emerge was a commitment in all of our programs to ensure that the content of classes and workshops dealt seriously with issues of race, class, and sex as they are expressed in the life of our communities and our congregations. The faculty made a self-conscious effort to examine its own expressions of sexism, working on each other's unfortunate use of language, blindness to our own failures, and our continuing to maintain traditional male attitudes. One result of growing sensitivity was the requirement that classroom papers from students must use inclusive language.

Finally, major attention was given to developing patterns of evaluation. Our program budget form made it easy to understand the cost and scope of each individual program. At the same time, the trustees were insistent that for the wide-ranging program pattern we were developing we set up careful and rigorous evaluation procedures. These were worked out over several years with considerable help from experienced professional evaluators. The result was the requirement that for every new academic program clear goals had to be set forth against which results could be measured. Then details of the curriculum and requirements were drawn up, with a commitment by faculty and students to utilize the evaluation process. Each June the faculty spent half a day or more examining the evaluation reports for each program checking to see if the programs had met expectations and were within our budget allocations. A similar evaluation procedure was followed for each individual class.

Each faculty member was also subjected to an evaluation process undertaken (in cooperation) by other members of the administrative faculty. A thorough evaluation form was designed. All members of the faculty would fill out the forms for their colleagues and themselves. As the process unfolded, we developed the pattern of two-year contracts, with individuals being thoroughly evaluated in February of the year that their contracts expired. This meant that approximately half the faculty were subjected to this routine each academic year. Summaries were then shared among the faculty. This was followed up by a several-hour conversation with the individuals. This joint process, however, followed an intensive interview of each individual by the chief executive officer who at that point was in a position to make a decision with regard to a contract renewal. The meeting with the joint faculty, which presupposed rehiring, focused on developing faculty relationships and improving the competence of the faculty member under review.

The Long-Range Planning and Transition Program

The period from 1975–79 ended with the decision to undertake both long-range planning and the transition to election and seating of a new chief executive officer. The story begins back a bit further, however. I had become increasingly sensitive about the degree to which much of the developing life of the seminary had been dependent on my own particular style. I was extensively involved in the program and academic life of the seminary as well as assuming the normal responsibilities of a seminary president. It seemed unlikely that my successor would find it fulfilling or compatible to function in any comparable way. So I began to mull over how a responsible transition could be planned. This reflection was nudged along by certain events. One was the appearance on my desk of a newspaper clipping reporting that a major college president had said, "In this day and age eight years is as long as anyone can be expected to function effectively as a chief executive officer of an institution of higher learning." Some trustee would occasionally make a joke about what would happen to the seminary if Webber got hit by a truck. There was a certain awareness of the variety of things I kept in my own portfolio that made the seminary very vulnerable and pointed to the need for some protective measures. I also was aware of the fact that the founder of the seminary, W. W. White, had remained as president as he grew senile, thus creating a host of problems for the institution.

A significant development came in the fall of 1978. We had made a substantial funding request to the Arthur Vining Davis Foundations. About the first of December, the foundation executive, who clearly was supportive of the seminary, called to say that she had been looking at our material but somehow it didn't seem to add up to something the foundation could support. She had an interesting suggestion, however. We had been functioning for nine years under the new style. Did it make sense to take time now to do a comprehensive self-study of what the seminary was about and to undertake extensive planning that would help us prepare for the future while keeping intact what was important from the past? We responded with enthusiasm and very real appreciation. But it occurred to me at once that such a process would have a lot more teeth and considerably more integrity if I were to indicate to the trustees my desire to terminate my presidency at its conclusion. So I suggested that the trustees, in approving the grant from the Arthur Vining Davis Foundations and committing themselves to such an extensive self-study, also recognize that I was submitting my resignation to be effective at a time that met the best interests of the seminary but in no case later than June 30, 1983—four more years. Once my colleagues and the trustees were clear that this was not done out of anger but from a real commitment to the future of the seminary, I think they all agreed it was a good idea and that we should get to work on the self-study.

At the same time we were strengthened by an inquiry from the National Executive Service Corps (NESC) as to whether the seminary would be interested in making use of their resources. This organization had for years made available to non-profit organizations the voluntary help of top corporate executives. They had worked frequently with colleges and universities but never with a theological seminary. Robert Lynn of the Lilly Endowment had talked at some length about this with Frank Pace, the head of NESC, and had agreed that Lilly would pay the modest fee required if we wanted to arrange a consultation for the seminary. In the course of some very hard-hitting interviews, I was forced to become more specific about seminary problems related to our administrative structure, our financial picture, and the role of the trustees. NESC then offered us the part-time assistance for six months of one or two appropriate executives now retired who could provide us with consultation help in understanding and solving issues in these areas. The person assigned had to be mutually acceptable, that is, there had to be proper chemistry between the person and the institution. And in fact this proved to be the case with the selection of Fred Richards, who had recently retired after many years as a corporate executive. An active Presbyterian layman, he brought genuine interest in the work of the seminary with the kind of wisdom and perspective we found invaluable.

Finally, the transition process was encouraged by a new program of the Lilly Endowment to provide seminaries with fund-raising expertise through helping them employ and train a development officer. This offer was made to us in the spring of 1979. By September 1, we had located as our development officer-in-training Carolyn Hopley. She had recently graduated from Union Theological Seminary with a master of divinity degree and was willing to undertake this specialized ministry.

Over the following two years she was given excellent training through the resources of the Lilly Endowment.

Thus we began the period of long-range planning and the transition to the selection and seating of a new chief executive officer.

Conclusion

These years of both stability and change ended with graduation on May 20, 1979, and, for me, with a sense of great gratitude for my first ten years at the seminary and with some anticipation as well as anxiety about the transition that lay ahead. I took the occasion of my closing remarks at the graduation to reflect a bit on what the seminary is all about:

> As a Christmas greeting to our friends last year we sent out a card with the words of Jeremiah in the 29th chapter: "Seek the welfare of the city where I have sent you into exile, and pray to the Lord on its behalf, for in its welfare you will find your welfare." For several years now, this text had focused our task as a seminary in the heart of New York City. As Christians, we know that we do march to the beat of a different drum, that our commitments and values stand over against the styles and values that our society seems to prize. But even when we feel like exiles in our own land, Jeremiah reminds us that we find our lives not in escape or rebellion, but precisely in seeking the shalom, the peace, of this incredible city.
>
> As we shape our task as an educational institution, we sense an urgency in being signs of shalom on 29th Street, in showing forth those signs of the kingdom that are reflections of how God has called God's children to live and work. Jesus announced loud and clear that, for his followers, the kingdom was now. But we need to move from rhetoric to specifics. In what sense can we seek to be witnesses to the kingdom, signs of shalom that challenge, provoke, and fascinate the city around us? In three ways at least.
>
> 1. *As a sign of the unity Christ brings.* In Christ there is neither Jew nor Greek, rich or poor, male or female, white, Hispanic or black, but we are made to know again that we are

brothers and sisters. The sociology of our day makes it almost impossible for any local congregation to reflect this incredible truth that simply shatters the common wisdom that keeps races and classes apart. New York Theological Seminary is unique in its incredibly diverse student body, reflecting the entire spectrum of the Christian churches, cutting across racial and class divisions as well. Of the 412 students enrolled in a substantial program, twenty percent are white clergy, fifty percent are black, and thirty percent Hispanic, reflecting every neighborhood in the metropolitan area from exclusive suburb to inner city. Even as we rejoice in our opportunity, we struggle against our own racism and seek to open ourselves to the gifts such diverse brothers and sisters bring to our lives.

2. *We are a sign of the kingdom when we are an educational community that challenges the students not simply to gain more knowledge, but to grow toward maturity in Christ, to the full stature God calls them to discover in their lives.* Such a community means hard work, discipline, the pain of growth that comes when cherished ideas are threatened and new insights demand new ways of work and witness. We are faithful when our students grow in knowledge, but more importantly, in maturity as God's children and in competence in God's ministry.

3. *Finally, we are a sign of shalom when our students begin to take seriously their callings to care for the city.* So often, ministry is seen as caring for a congregation, meeting the needs of one's members. But clearly, Christ sets us free to take care of this world, to be a Christ to one's neighbor. God's church is turned inside out, witnessing to the kingdom just as Jesus did, by healing the sick, helping the blind to see, setting at liberty the prisoner, and living now in the day of our Lord. Our clergy are precious people, called by God to leadership in working for peace and justice in this city. The seminary is a sign of shalom when its students take up the challenge, and with their people, "Seek the welfare of the city."

Our faithfulness as an institution, our effectiveness, needs continually to be tested by the degree to which these signs of shalom are made visible here as gifts from God.

CHAPTER 4

A Time of Transition

1979–1983

During the years from 1969–79 New York Theological Seminary experienced a dramatic recovery from a long period of declining health. The decision made in March, 1970, to terminate the master of divinity degree had made possible a major reordering of seminary staffing, financing, and program emphases.[1] Whereas in the world of accredited seminaries the focus was on training college graduates for ministries in the churches or in teaching, NYTS was offering programs for church leaders, lay and ordained, who wished to undertake theological studies at any level from non-accredited Saturday studies, through college work, to formal level seminary programs leading to an MDiv or DMin. The fact that we were not on a crusade to reform traditional patterns of theological education, as for example was the INTER-MET program in Washington, meant that we did not have to waste energy fighting the theological education

1. See Monograph V: *The Finances of New York Theological Seminary.*

"establishment" nor did we generate unnecessary hostility. We were just different (or perhaps perceived as peculiar) and able to respond to a variety of requests that would usually be seen as inappropriate for a seminary. Accepting students only on the basis of part-time study, with classes primarily in the evening or on weekends, appealing almost entirely to persons over thirty years of age, with a student body predominantly black and Hispanic, operating out of rented space on an incredibly low budget, we threatened no one, competed with no other seminary, and were given space to grow and develop in our unique ways.

Over 500 students were enrolled in programs that required at a minimum one year of study, but averaged four to six years. For those wishing simply to learn more about faith there was the certificate program, requiring attendance for twenty-eight Saturdays from 9 A.M. to 3 P.M. The accredited college program was enrolling about 200 students, most of whom attended classes two evenings each week, right through the year. Graduate level seminary programs (master of professional studies, master of divinity, master of sacred theology and doctor of ministry) made up the third ring of study options and attracted a wide range of metropolitan area clergy seeking continuing education to enhance their ministries and an increasing number of mature lay persons seeking the credentials for ordination.

To a large extent, the new shape evolved as the seminary administration was able to respond to clearly articulated needs from prospective students and broker effective programs. There was a powerful sense of the leading of the spirit, suggesting that gratitude rather than pride was the proper stance for us all. By God's grace we had been provided with facilities, adequate funding, competent, risk-taking faculty, and an exciting and challenging range of students who sought from us the knowledge, faith, understanding, and competence in practice that would enable them better to seek the shalom of the communities where they had been called to ministry.

But now our sense of having been led by the spirit, of taking one year at a time, was tempered by the realization that we had entered into a time of transition. The reality that new leadership had to be found gave urgency and a sense of reality to the realization that long-range planning, an effort to give thought and direction to the future, could be undertaken in legitimate tension with our previous freedom to respond and experiment. When the Arthur Vining Davis Foundations suggested that they might be willing to help fund such an evaluation process, faculty and trustees agreed that, since the seminary had succeeded in establishing new traditions and developing considerable momentum, it could now well afford time for the evaluation and planning that would give coherence and direction for the years ahead. There were three major phases to this period of transition.

The Self-Study and Development of the Long-Range Plan

In the late spring of 1979 three outside consultants were asked to read over seminary documents: Larry Mamiya from Vassar College, Parker Palmer of Pendle Hill, and Barbara Wheeler of Auburn seminary. They then spent a day with trustees and faculty to help design a process for the self-study and long-range planning committee; this was held in June, 1979. This was followed by a full-day faculty/trustee meeting at the end of July. The work was undergirded by the consultant from the National Executive Service Corps and the new full-time development trainee. We all recognized that New York Theological Seminary had a unique opportunity to undertake educational ministries unhampered by many of the traditional restraints imposed on most theological seminaries. We thus had a strong obligation to use our freedom and flexibility to the best possible ends. Having operated for ten years without much attention to our administration patterns, we now needed to get a fix on our present position and to give thought to our goals, styles, and funding for the years ahead.

The planning committee assumed the task of creating a long-range document that would provide the seminary with a clear picture of the present operation plans for the future and a program for their implementation. The elements for such a document were defined under six headings, each with a task force designed to give attention to that area. They were described in the document as follows:

1. Evaluation of our present educational program leading to the details of a functioning program of ongoing evaluation for all elements of the seminary and for continuing planning;
2. Clear understanding of what we seek in terms of the role of trustees and how we can achieve such a membership;
3. Agreement on the basic goals and purposes of the seminary with strategies for achieving them;
4. A carefully defined and initially implemented development program;
5. Development of an appropriate and efficient administrative structure and support services;
6. The job description and profile of the next president and a program for selection and transition.

Details of the processes by which each of these task forces undertook its work are given in Appendix C. It is sufficient to say here that a team of several trustees, faculty, alumni, and students was assigned to each major task.

The initial assignment fell to the Task Force on Purposes and Priorities. Its attempt to develop a clear statement of the self-understanding of the seminary in terms of its focus and purpose was important as the bench mark by which the other task forces could judge the relevance of what they were doing. The committee sought to test its initial statement with a wide range of students, alumni, and faculty as well as trustees. A similar statement had been made in 1973 and the task force used that document as the basis for revision and redrafting rather than starting from scratch. The results of its work, officially accepted at a trustee meeting, was then used by the other task forces. (See Appendix C.) Several important elements of the statement reflected a growing self-awareness in the seminary community of its essential tasks. It had become clear that "The Seminary's primary student body are the women and men of this metropolitan area who have made a commitment to Jesus Christ and are engaged in some form of ministry through their church or secular work." A strong new emphasis was apparent in this: "Faculty and students together seek to relate educational programs to different experiences of oppression, particularly those based on race, sex, and class, and to support one another to work for the alleviation of injustice." At the same time, the heritage was affirmed in this statement: ". . . in carrying out these purposes we will emphasize biblical competence as an essential in being equipped for ministry."

One critical element in this process was our extensive use of consultants. The initial design had been significantly shaped with their help. Now we had the services of Fred Richards, a retired corporate executive, and Alan Green with his long experience as a foundation executive, educational consultant, and development expert. Fred Richards was assigned to the Task Force on Trustees and Development. I had been very nervous about how such an outside business person would respond to the functioning of the seminary. It was with relief that we received from him a strong affirmation of the basic composition of our trustees. Whereas according to common wisdom trustees of a theological seminary should be distinguished clergy and lay persons, preferably with financial resources, the seminary had sought trustees from a wide range of people reflecting the diversity of our constituency, thus providing credibility for the many different groups that were seeking to use our resources. Richards attended trustee meetings and consulted with individual members of the board. He helped the task force at several points, more by confirming ideas that were already developing than by counseling any significant departures. It was his suggestion that led us to read a series of pamphlets by Robert Greenleaf with his emphasis upon servanthood as the image for the trustee and for a seminary. Out of this study came the commitment by the chairperson of the board to take primary responsibility for nurturing its morale and work rather than counting upon the chief executive officer to assume that responsibility as had hitherto largely been the case. This task force also came up with the idea of a covenant for the trustees that would indicate annually their commitment to the seminary and the work of its trustees as well as the seminary's responsibility to them.

Fred Richard's primary work was with the Development Committee. For the first time, a development officer trainee was at work full-time, providing major new energy to complement the president's efforts. One disturbing issue emerged very quickly: the seminary received a remarkably high percentage of its income from tuition, but had very limited endowment resources; it had been financially viable over the previous nine years due largely to foundation grants. Such a high level of grants could not be expected to continue indefinitely. We recognized not only that foundations were reluctant to give to any one institution on a continuing basis, but also that the number of foundations interested in religion in general and theological education in particular were extremely limited, and there was little evidence that seminary support would be a priority even for these. Thus our dependence on such grants made us particularly vulnerable for the immediate future. As a part of his early assignment, Fred Richards introduced me to the grants officers of several large corporations with an interest in New York City. By the end of our fifth interview, it had become clear that, on the whole, corporations do not give to religious causes and, though fascinated by some of our programs, were unable to consider support of a Protestant theological seminary. It was Fred Richards who pointed out that much of our energy was devoted to helping equip urban leaders for a more effective role in the life of their communities. Why not, he suggested, create a separate fund that could receive grants for empowering urban leaders, rather than for religious or theological training. Out of this came a proposal for a Fund for Black and Hispanic Leadership Development in New York City. Within a year and a half, the fund had been incorporated and was granted a 501(C)3 status by the Internal Revenue Service. We made the purpose of this fund very clear. It was a device for separating funds to be used primarily for enhancing the capacities of our students for public leadership as opposed to sacerdotal functions. The board of the fund was made up primarily of seminary trustees and others who understood that these funds were primarily to help meet the budget of a specific seminary program. Our use of a program budget that made implicit the allocation of funds for particular elements of each program enabled us to demonstrate to potential givers precisely how we were using grants for the Fund for Black and Hispanic Leadership Development.

Although Fred Richards' voluntary services were only for a six-month period, they were invaluable, not only in terms of their specific results, but because of his outsider's perspective on what we were about, his ability to ask questions that were penetrating and challenging but which did not create any defensiveness on our part, and the variety of suggestions he offered that would not have occurred to those of us who were so directly involved in the life of the institution.

The other consultant, Alan Green, spent a number of days on three separate occasions sharing in the life of the seminary, talking to members of the faculty and staff, and then offering us his own reflections and ideas. On one occasion he spent two days at our annual faculty retreat at a Catholic center near Beacon, New York. On another occasion Green was asked to read over the description of one of our degree programs and then by talking with students, alumni, and instructors evaluate what we were actually doing in terms of that program. His insights about our administrative faculty were particularly helpful. Over the years both faculty and trustees had spent a good deal of time and energy debating whether we ought to continue the practice by which administrative faculty were expected for the most part to have some commitment to ministry outside the life of the seminary. It seemed to me as CEO that it would be good to have a small group of colleagues whose energy was almost entirely focused on the life of the seminary. At the same time there were arguments for our faculty having a unique relationship with the life of the local congregations and community. Alan Green strongly recommended that faculty be employed on a full-time basis while continuing to encourage their vital participation in the life of a congregation. Green went on to describe his view of what should be required of NYTS faculty:

> My recommendation respecting the kinds of people you want in these administrative faculty positions is that they be

> primarily teachers with low control needs, with solid urban pastoral or social agency experience, and with completed higher degree aspirations and demonstrated commitment to continued learning from others, from the environment, and from literary sources. They should be people who do not hope for lifetime careers at NYTS or any other seminary, but see their work at the seminary as an episode in a personal pilgrimage that might include returning to, or entering, the parish ministry, counseling, political office, one of the professions, business, trade unions, civil service, or retirement. Finally, they should all be to some extent bilingual, at least within one year of joining the faculty, and should know something about Hispanic/Caribbean cultures, the culture of black Americans, Korean culture, or that of any group represented in significant numbers at the seminary.

This, of course, is a dream sheet, but one aspect of the uniqueness of NYTS is its openness to many different realities. The more open the administrative faculty can be to the cultures, occupations, and experiences of other individuals and groups, the better the chance that this openness will be maintained and modeled for the seminary's students.

This turned out to be precisely the direction in which the seminary would in fact move, leading to a core faculty of ten to twelve. What did not change was the assumption about priorities. The core faculty would not give primary attention to scholarship and teaching but would combine, in a very demanding way, administration, teaching, involvement in the life of the church, and contributions to the ongoing life and thought of the community through lecturing and writing. Only the professor of biblical studies, as part of the position contract, was given a significant block of time for scholarly research and writing.

Much of the work of the long-range planning committee had been fully accomplished by the summer of 1981 with the final report ready for thorough discussion at the annual trustees/faculty overnight retreat in January 1982. By this time, the board of trustees had already taken a number of actions dealing with problem areas that had arisen and with laying the foundation for the administrative structure for subsequent years. We needed a policy on our dispersed degree programs. The trustees had been rather nervous about our willingness to respond to needs far from New York City, such as our long-term work in Maine and the DMin program in England. This hardly seemed in line with our basic policy of meeting the needs of laity and clergy in the metropolitan area of New York City. The ATS was also troubled about the proliferation of dispersed programs in the seminary. In order to give some focus and clarity to these programs and to prevent one or other of the deans from seeking to respond to any cry for help no matter from how far afield, the seminary took a look both as its justification for these programs and the guidelines of the ATS. Clearly we needed a policy statement. The following statement was confirmed by the trustees in their meeting in May, 1981, following two or three earlier drafts.

Policy Statement Regarding Dispersed Programs

I. Definition

Dispersed programs are those programs offered by New York Theological Seminary where the student body and primary base of operation is outside the New York metropolitan area (for example, outside of New York City and the thirteen adjoining counties). Examples of present dispersed programs include Washington, D.C., and the British DMin programs; Maine STM in parish ministry, and Trinity (Princeton, N.J.) STM in counseling.

II. Programs will be considered that meet the following conditions (in toto):

A. We will seek to fulfill the spirit of the recommendations of the Association of Theological Schools in the United States and Canada. A copy of these guidelines is appended.
B. The students have no other viable option available, and New York Theological Seminary has available adequate resources to meet the need.
C. The students are able to attend the seminary for a significant educational component (as with the Maine STM and the two DMin programs).

D. The program will cover the costs incurred by New York Theological Seminary in full, including an appropriate overhead allocation.
E. Out-of-state governmental agency approval can be obtained where required.
F. Competent and appropriate NYTS qualified faculty are available.
G. It does not absorb more than a limited amount (say one-third) of the Dean's energy nor enroll more than one-third of the student quota for any program.
H. The specific goals and evaluation procedures for the program are outlined in detail and carefully processed in order to insure a quality program.
I. From the beginning a clear description of the program, its administrative structure, the specific budget, and other necessary details are outlined thoroughly and approved by the faculty and trustees.

This statement had the effect of restraining our impulse to respond as quickly as in the past and eventually led to phasing out the work in Maine.

Another area of concern that quickly emerged was the question of how large the seminary ought to become. A number of us had a strong feeling that at a certain quantitative point, a qualitative difference appears in an institution, and that the seminary should be very careful to maintain its style of collegiality and openness that could certainly be threatened if the institution grew too large. I was personally relieved when the trustees decided that the administrative faculty should be limited to ten to twelve persons and that the seminary's program should not outgrow the facilities that it was presently renting. While that left a fair amount of flexibility, it did suggest that we had already just about arrived at the limits to growth and would have to exercise great care in adding any new undertakings unless current programs were cut back.

This section might well be summed up by the answer that the faculty as a whole sent to the long-range planning committee when asked what they considered would be the essential character of the seminary in the years ahead. Assuming our commitment to our current location, independent ecumenical nature, and accreditation status, we suggested the following as essential to maintaining the present character of the seminary:

1. Our teaching, curriculum development, and overall life needs to be biblically centered.
2. We remain committed to a pluralistic constituency that includes all ethnic and racial groups, degree and non-degree students, and is representative of the diverse church life of the metropolitan area.
3. We remain church centered.
4. We maintain a clear commitment both to social justice issues and to the need for social change.
5. We continue our current form and style of governance, which is collegial and involves a shared partnership between the president, faculty, and trustees.
6. We are flexible in order to respond to emerging needs and new program initiatives.

All of this might be summed up by saying that essential to continuing the current character of the seminary is a commitment to education that is oriented to the needs of both clergy and laity, and that is praxis based and church centered. This educational enterprise is pursued in a collegial style with a heavy emphasis on shared leadership and decision making.

The Profile of the President

The second major element of these transition years was the development of a job description for the new president. Clearly one of the prime reasons for the self-study was to get a good grasp on what would be required of a new chief executive officer. I had done a careful time-study during several different periods of an academic year and had tried to draw up a comprehensive description of what I was currently doing and how much time had to be allocated for each task. This was by no means a definitive description of the new president's job. I think we all took it for granted that my present allocation of time was largely a function of my own style and personality rather than what was necessarily required by the job. For example, there was no reason to assume that the new president would want to give as much time to teaching and academic administration as I had done, nor that my particular pattern of fund-raising should be determinative for the future.

The final job description emerged from a fairly lengthy process in which faculty, students, trustees, and alumni were all asked both in person and through questionnaires for their thoughts on what should be required in the new chief executive officer. The end product, which was then circulated in the academic year 1981–82, read as follows:

WANTED

PRESIDENT FOR
NEW YORK THEOLOGICAL SEMINARY

An urban, interracial, interdenominational seminary with a strong biblical tradition, committed to the training and education of clergy and laity active in ministry. Located in midtown Manhattan, the seminary has a student population of 350.

The president is responsible to the board of trustees for the overall administration and exercises this responsibility collegially with an administrative faculty of ten.

Requirements:

1. Pastor-theologian with an earned doctorate and experience in urban ministry;
2. Demonstrated ability in administration, fund-raising, and public relations;
3. Commitment to social justice with priority to transforming those structures that impede justice;
4. Teaching experience, familiarity with nontraditional, innovative education, with an emphasis on an action/reflection model of theological education;
5. Demonstrated ability to function in cross-cultural and interracial situations.

Other Considerations:

1. Knowledge of and sensitive to continuance of firm ecumenical relations and demonstrated ability to work with various denominations and traditions;
2. Compassion toward and understanding of the needs of a seminary community;
3. Skills in management, evaluation, and budgeting;
4. Knowledge of Spanish language;
5. Publications.

Compensation: Negotiable

Starting Date: No later than July 1, 1983

This job description was carefully considered by the subcommittee on the transition of the long-range planning committee before being widely distributed. A search committee made up of nineteen persons who reflected the constituency of the seminary was then appointed. There were four trustees, three faculty, three students, three alumni, and several representatives of the administrative staff. I was not a voting member, but was occasionally used as a consultant and was present at the final meeting where the new president was elected. The chairperson of the committee was a Baptist layman and long-time trustee, Carl Fields Jr.

The list of prospective candidates eventually numbered over fifty, with suggestions coming from theological educators, ordained clergy, denominational executives, and secular educators. A strong effort was made to find women candidates. The most obvious dynamic was generated by the administrative faculty, who had a very great vested interest in the outcome. At the beginning several members indicated their personal interest in the position and hope that they might discuss their availability with the search committee. Their interest was openly considered in faculty meetings, but no clear consensus emerged, at least at the early stages, as to whether one of the faculty would be the appropriate choice. What could have been a very divisive issue seemed to have been handled with maturity by both the candidates and their colleagues.

I am not clear about one dynamic that seemed to emerge in the process. I had the strong impression that our Hispanic constituency was troubled by the thought of having a black president, while our black constituency expressed some subtle concern about the possibility of having an Hispanic president. This led me to reflect on the degree to which our pluralistic community could best be held together by a president who came from neither of these two groups but who was surrounded by strong and able colleagues who had the confidence of both communities. In any case, as the search committee narrowed its list to six or seven candidates, the administrative faculty coalesced around one person.

Keith Russell had not considered himself as in any way a candidate. He was finding fulfillment in combining his role as a pastor in Brooklyn with teaching at the seminary as part of the administrative faculty. Only after much prodding by his colleagues and a good deal of prayer and discussion with his family did he consent to stand as a candidate. The fact that he was not pushing himself forward for the job gave him a certain freedom and objectivity when he was interviewed by the search committee, which found this very attractive. At the end of the day, the choice was between Keith Russell, whom the seminary community knew and trusted, and a very able and distinguished graduate of Biblical Seminary who had subsequently pursued a doctoral degree in biblical studies, had served as pastor of a congregation for some years and was currently a professor and administrator at a midwestern university. His interviews had been very strong and he had impressed the search committee with his remarkable qualifications, his Christian commitment, and his very real interest in returning to his alma mater.

I was present at the final meeting of the search committee where the qualifications of the two candidates were thoroughly discussed. Toward the end we had an impressive speech from an Hispanic female trustee who had an important administrative post as well as a professorship at an urban university. She said something to the effect that the alumnus was a wonderful academic administrator with all the qualifications that one might hope for in a seminary president in terms of experience, academic credentials, and the like. She indicated she would be delighted to work under him in her own university. But she went on to say, "Keith has one thing that is precious. We know that he is thoroughly trusted by the black and Hispanic communities and is able to work with us with sensitivity and compassion. This is a gift that no experience will produce, and thus I'm convinced that he is our man. He lacks much of the experience that the other person has. We can teach him those things. There's no way you can guarantee that the other candidate will be able to win the kind of trust that Keith has already gained." With that the decision was settled and Keith was selected unanimously as the nominee to the trustees. Several weeks later at a special meeting of the board of trustees he was elected president.

New Developments

During these four transition years, several new challenges demanded a response. In the spring of 1981, Ed Muller, a Methodist pastor who had served for more than fifteen years as a chaplain in the New York State prison system, came to see me along with Karel Boersma, a young clergyman of the Christian Reformed Church who had been volunteering a day a week at Greenhaven Prison. They had an idea that demanded attention. They told me that over 400 long-term prisoners in various correctional facilities in New York State had been able to acquire an accredited degree through extension programs from nearby colleges. Many of these men had a very strong faith, either Christian or Muslim, and were eager to continue higher education. So Muller and Boersma had come to ask the seminary to create a graduate degree program for such prisoners. This was the most unconventional idea that had been proposed to the seminary since I had come there. As we discussed the possibilities thoroughly, I came to feel that it would not be difficult for us to shape such a program if it were held at some nearby prison and we were able to recruit really serious students. The problem was not the ability of the seminary to mount such a program, but the inevitable reluctance of the state correctional system to permit it. Muller and Boersma went away convinced that the seminary would be most responsive to sponsoring such a program, but that it was up to them to convince the prison system bureaucracy that it was feasible, and more importantly, desirable.

Here again grace entered the picture. It happened that the deputy commissioner responsible for ministerial and family services in the state prisons was Earl Moore. He had received his STM in pastoral counseling at New York Theological Seminary and several years later completed his doctor of ministry with us while serving as both pastor of a church in Harlem and deputy commissioner in the correctional system. His DMin project had been to develop more effective family services for those in state prisons. Moore responded with enthusiasm to the proposal for such a continuing education program and was determined to do everything in his power to gain the necessary permission and cooperation. Only his presence gave us any chance of pulling it off. We already had authorization from the state to offer a thirty-six credit master of professional studies. We decided to use that nomenclature to offer a degree in prison ministry designed for college graduates with a strong religious commitment. I wrote up a draft curriculum that would provide the prisoner-students with the insight, knowledge, and skills to work as lay pastors as long as they remained in the prison system.

Our plan was relatively simple. Eligible men would be transferred to a convenient prison and be assigned as full-time students. Each morning we would send a competent professor for a semester long course covering the basic theological disciplines and practical skills required in their ministry. Thus they would have on Monday morning, Bible; Tuesday, church history; Wednesday, theology; Thursday, a reflection group; and Friday, pastoral counseling. The afternoons would be spent in what amounted to field work, assisting in various forms of service in the prison. The evenings would provide time for disciplined study.

The package sounded very neat. The problems proved to be immense. The initial design was drawn up in the fall of 1981. Then began the long process of securing the necessary permissions from the state correctional system director, the divisions responsible for education, and from the superintendent of Sing Sing, thirty miles north of New York City, which had been selected as the base. Such a program violated the basic ethos of the correctional system. In spite of the term "correctional," the prison system in this country exists primarily to punish criminals. There is little sympathy for providing incarcerated men with opportunities for education. For the most part, those who serve as guards are troubled by prisoners receiving such a break, even at the college level. The idea that long-term criminals would be allowed to go to graduate school must have seemed to many people completely out of bounds. But Dr. Moore was equal to the challenge. I remember going with him on his first visit to the superintendent at Sing Sing and those responsible for education programs in the prison system. The superintendent, a very able administrator, clearly was not enthusiastic about having his present work complicated further by another program. He indicated that the extensive remodeling currently underway at his facility made it almost impossible to provide space and that there were other problems. However, once he discovered that the decision had been made at the top that the program was going forward and that it would be at Sing Sing, he became cooperative and supportive of what we were doing.

However, approval of the program in principle did not solve all the problems. Recruitment was slow, as the seminary was totally dependent on word getting out to chaplains in the facilities scattered all over New York State. Qualifications were restrictive. Applicants had to have an accredited college degree, be attested to by the chaplain and others in their respective facility as having a clear and meaningful religious commitment, accept transfer to Sing Sing (not a desirable location for long-term prisoners), agree to continue in the program for the eleven months it would require without accepting any early parole, and give primary attention to their educational program and its commitments, which meant that visitors would be limited to weekends. Our agreement involved the transfer of the students to Sing Sing by July 1, with orientation and preparation for classes to begin the first week in September. Karel Boersma was hired as the coordinator of the program to spend several days a week at the facility. However, as the summer dragged on, the applications were held up, and transfers were bogged down. We postponed the beginning date to August 1, then to September 1, and were fully prepared to abort the whole program when it finally fell into place about the middle of September. We had secured an excellent faculty who were blessed with the patience to hold open the time for us until we were finally able to begin at the end of September. Church history was taught by a professor from Maryknoll Seminary, located in Ossining, and the Bible by a black scholar/pastor from Montclair, New Jersey. Pastoral counseling seminars were led by an Hispanic pastor from East Harlem, and the theology course was taught by another Hispanic scholar on our own faculty, Sam Solivan.

The problem of financing was implicit from the very beginning. I had quite confidently told the proposers of the program that we would find the money somehow. Several efforts in the spring of 1982, however, had been unsuccessful. At the trustee meeting in May, when there seemed a strong likelihood the project would get underway and had to be approved, I had in my usual pattern suggested to the trustees that they vote the project with the proviso that it proceed only if money could be found. To my surprise, for the first time in my experience, the trustees voted independently of whether we had substantial funds on hand to go ahead with the program, with the confidence that we would find the money somehow. By August 1, however, I had not come up with anything. The day before I left on my vacation, one of our MDiv students, an older businessman who was now planning on a second career in ministry to alcoholics, came by for a talk. I was describing the program to him with no thought of asking for funds when he said, "you've got $5,000." That unexpected gift gave me a little confidence that we would indeed find the funds. And that proved to be the case in subsequent months. Individuals, congregations, and foundations were stirred by the imagination of the program, and before the end of December, we found the total amount necessary to cover the cost of the first year.

A second challenge, this time laid primarily before the president-in-training, was related to our joint program with New Brunswick Theological Seminary. After 1980, the number of students in the program had increased dramatically. We had originally thought in terms of about fifteen new students each year with perhaps fifty enrolled at any one time; in fact we had in the neighborhood of forty entering students with a total of one hundred enrolled in the normal MDiv student body at New Brunswick. This placed a tremendous strain on our available resources. Furthermore, there were certain inherent tensions in the pattern that had emerged between the two institutions. In effect, NYTS recruited the students and provided much of the work of their first year through the powerful experience of our integration seminars. Those were conducted primarily with communities of eight or nine students who worked intensively for four hours a week throughout the year, each with one of our administrative faculty. Then these students who had demonstrated their ability to do solid graduate MDiv work were passed along to New Brunswick. Although we continued to offer courses and relate to the students as advisors, they basically moved under the umbrella of New Brunswick. It began to feel less like the partnership that it had been in the early years when we were planning and cooperating very closely. The nine regular members of the New Brunswick faculty were expected to teach one semester a year in our evening program, thus requiring a commute to NYTS. This was a considerable sacrifice on their part, since it meant getting home very late at night after a wearying train ride. The problem was that, whereas forty percent or more of our students were women, the New Brunswick faculty was all male. Only one was not a member of the Reformed Church of America. So our diverse student body—only one or two of whom were from that denomination and perhaps five percent from the Reformed tradition as a whole—was receiving most of its theological education within that context. No matter how hard the New Brunswick faculty tried to adjust to the diverse student body, they clearly were under severe limitations. To put it bluntly, only three or four of them were committed to the program and they did an excellent job. Several others tried but found it very difficult to teach in this context, and two or three were not enthusiastic at all and were ineffective in it.

The turning point came in the fall of 1981, one of the

professors who was teaching an introductory course to first-year students failed half the class and gave Cs to a good percentage of the rest. He simply had been unwilling to meet the students where they were and had demanded that they fit into his whole pattern of thinking and teaching. The situation became even more distressing when that spring the same students took a class with one of his colleagues who gave eighty percent of the class either As or Bs. Something simply had to be done. I talked with the coordinator of the program about the need to develop a genuinely cooperative and collegial pattern. New Brunswick was very receptive to this idea. We planned to set up a joint team to administer the MDiv program, with New Brunswick and NYTS as equal partners. We proposed to use a diverse group of faculty and to plan the whole curriculum jointly, rather than NYTS just passing the students on to New Brunswick after the first year. This would obviously mean a good deal more work for both institutions, but it seemed a much more creative way to respond to the needs of our student constituency than the former arrangements. The new agreement went into effect in the fall of 1982. An immediate issue erupted. I had been dean of the program on behalf of New York Theological Seminary but would be resigning as president at the end of the academic year. Our faculty became convinced that this offered a wonderful opportunity to bring in as dean on our behalf a first-rate black scholar who would fill a serious gap in the composition of the NYTS faculty. Whether this person would serve as dean of our joint program or as the representative of the seminary on the administrative team had not been decided, but either option was clearly practical. At that point a very unfortunate misunderstanding occurred that had dramatic consequences. As dean for our new joint program, the New Brunswick faculty decided to recommend a young Hispanic member of their faculty who had been working in the program for several years. NYTS had thought we would engage in an open search for the best possible person, and, considering our constituency, that priority would be given to a black scholar. When New Brunswick conveyed to us their recommendation in the form of a decision that sounded like an ultimatum, we were thrown into considerable confusion, not to say shock. At that point, Keith Russell, Vice President Bill Weisenbach, and I asked ourselves three questions: Was it possible for NYTS to mount its own MDiv program? Could we do a better academic job than the joint program in terms of the needs of our students? And would it be possible to secure accreditation from the Association of Theological Schools? Our conclusion was an unambiguous affirmative to each of these questions. Clearly, we could develop our own program. We would be able to call upon a much more diverse faculty than a singly denominational school, one that would reflect the various traditions from which our students came, and offer a curriculum focusing very specifically on their needs.

Our ability to achieve accreditation was somewhat more problematic, but it seemed feasible. Then we had another real break. To mount a full MDiv program, we would require more space, much better library facilities, and additional faculty with solid credentials. With this in mind, Keith Russell made a visit to the dean of General Theological Seminary, about fourteen blocks away, with the request that our students have full access to its superb library, with our paying appropriate costs. He also asked to rent space for our evening classes with the idea that if our students actually had class there, we could justify their access to its first-rate theological library. Our third request was that several of General's professors teach courses in such fields as church history and New Testament, where we had no faculty of our own. Imagine Keith's great surprise when Dean Fenhagen acted as though he had come as an angel from heaven. It turned out that General had just been through a two-year racial audit examining the ways in which it was dealing with minority students and racial issues. The idea that our seminary with its large constituency of black and Hispanic students and faculty would join forces to some degree with General seemed to present a wonderful opportunity. Fenhagen went beyond meeting all of our requests: he suggested what we would never have had the temerity to propose; namely, that our institutions encourage free cross-registration. We felt confident that under these circumstances we could fully meet the accreditation expectations. Although General's daytime courses would not be available to many of our students, they would certainly provide tremendous enrichment for some and a strong resource as we did more corporate curriculum planning.

We now had the task of finding a first-rate scholar/administrator to serve as dean of our MDiv program. Several months of diligent search turned up no obvious candidate. One evening, one of our faculty, when talking with Professor Gayraud Wilmore at Colgate-Rochester Theological Seminary, laughingly suggested to Gay that if he had any desire to return to New York, he should explore our need for a dean of the MDiv program. The next morning Gay called to say that he and his wife had talked about this at great length and he would like to know more about the program. We had an emergency faculty meeting and voted without any hesitation to call this man whom we knew to be a scholar of outstanding reputation, a wonderful human being, and a great teacher. Shortly thereafter the trustees agreed with our recommendation. Thus began several months of intensive courtship on our part as we sought to deal with his questions and anxieties about making such a drastic break with his academic career and present responsibilities. With great joy we finally received his acceptance in midsummer. He began work at the beginning of the fall semester of 1983, gradually taking over responsibility from me. We were confident that the program was in good hands.

The Final Year of Transition

Even before his formal election as president, Keith had attended with me the biennial meeting of the Association of Theological Schools in the United States and Canada (ATS) held that year in Pittsburgh. While he was not introduced as president, I am sure that many people present suspected that he was the choice. More importantly, he was introduced to the life and dynamics of the association, and in particular, began to build relationships that would be important in subsequent years. He would have to deal with the Commission on Accrediting as the seminary sought to meet fully the ATS standards while continuing its wide range of unconventional programs.

A major source of support for this transition period came once again from the Arthur Vining Davis Foundations. They had supplied the grant that had made a long-range study possible and now were even more generous in providing funds that would enable us to bring Keith on a full presidential salary seven months prior to my relinquishing the position. During the fall he taught his regular part-time load. On December 1 he completed his work at the parish in Brooklyn and took up his position at the seminary as full-time president-in-training. During the next six months he assumed primary responsibility for planning for the coming academic year. He was the staff person largely responsible for working with the trustees in building the 1983–84 budget. He also had an opportunity to take some short-term courses that would help him with the various administrative tasks required of a CEO. I introduced him to foundation executives whose support would be crucial in subsequent years and gave him some clues on how I had gone about the overall task of development. His response to this period was tremendously encouraging, and I never wavered for a minute in my conviction that the seminary had been deeply blessed when it persuaded Keith to accept the presidency.

The actual passing of the baton came at graduation on May 22. Alan Green had early on suggested that we ought to indicate formally to our constituency that Keith was fully supported by those of us who had been responsible for the life of the seminary in the previous fourteen years and that we were confident that he would sustain the best of the past while being open to the continuing leading of the Spirit in the life of the seminary. As usual at graduation, the sanctuary at Marble Collegiate Church was packed. After I preached the graduation sermon, I gave Keith the symbols of office and my strongest blessing, with a great sense of confidence that the future was in good hands.

That evening, at our usual faculty party, there was an occasion to recognize the departing president and to welcome the new one. As a symbol of my time in office the faculty presented me with a case of scotch tape, equipment I had used to patch up many a problem at the seminary in the preceding years, and a gallon jar of olives, a staple that had been required at every event in the seminary's life where I was expected to be present.

During 1983–84 I continued to serve part-time both as a teacher, and as development officer with continuing responsibility for the basic fund-raising of the seminary. I did not attend administrative faculty meetings nor become involved directly in any of the primary policy-making situations. Every once in a while the other faculty would take a look at how Keith and I were doing and always came to the conclusion that Keith was clearly in charge and feeling quite confident about his responsibilities as chief executive officer.

During the academic year of 1984–85 we had a major accrediting visit by an ATS team. They kept asking people on the administration, faculty and staff rather oblique questions. It turned out they had been warned by the commission to expect to find Bill Webber still running the seminary from behind the scenes. As near as I can tell, everyone reassured them there had been no evidence of this even though during that academic year I had been reappointed to the administrative faculty, regularly attended meetings and took my own share of responsibility. My appointment that year, however, was only on a half-time basis while I spent two days a week as a consultant for the Boston Mission Society and taught a course at Harvard Divinity School.

From my point of view, the biggest change came in June, 1985 when Keith formally became the development officer and I reverted to being a consultant on development to him. I no longer had to assume major responsibility for fund-raising. It was the first time since I had been ordained in 1948 that I had not worked for some organization where if the bills were not paid I somehow felt it was my fault.

As I look around, many of my generation who have made a significant commitment to an institution or organization find on leaving their executive responsibilities that major changes occur, their contribution is quickly forgotten, and they feel rejected. At New York Theological Seminary, quite the reverse has been true. Keith Russell has built on the past, clearly is making his own unique and significant contribution, and is not at all threatened by the presence on the administrative faculty of his immediate predecessor. After nearly five years, I rejoice in his leadership and in remarkable new and creative developments that have emerged. He was clearly a superb choice.

EPILOGUE

Reflections from Distinguished Educators

When this manuscript was completed, President Keith Russell requested four outstanding educators to provide their comments on the story of New York Theological Seminary. Their thoughtful responses provide a helpful perspective that I am grateful to share with the reader.

Dr. Eldin Villafane

Director of the Center for Urban Ministerial Education, and Associate Professor of Christian Social Ethics Gordon-Conwell Theological Seminary

As a Puerto Rican pentecostal, whose church confession highlights the "leading of the Spirit," my heart is thrilled by the story of New York Theological Seminary under the leadership of George W. Webber. The story is "high drama," played out in a major northeastern metropolis. Its main actors involve an iconoclastic-prophetic theological educator pitted against, on one side by the traditional theological educational establishment, and on the other side by financial constraints and the fractured social fabric that defines its context.

It is a scenario in which the emergence of a "pilgrim seminary" becomes the dominant paradigm. One is indeed impressed by the "leading of the Spirit" as noted, especially, in its (l) philosophy of contextual theological education; (2) the primacy of its constituency focus; and (3) its programmatic development. The mix or dialectic of these three factors provided the richness and unique contribution of New York Theological Seminary.

Philosophy of Contextual Theological Education. One can speak of the shape of New York Theological Seminary as reflecting the interplay of both the "great personality" and "social dynamic" theories of history. Bill Webber's pilgrimage at Union Theological Seminary, East Harlem Protestant Parish, and the Metropolitan Urban Service Training (MUST), played a formative and critical role in the philosophy of education and ministry that was to emerge at NYTS. One should also mention the influence on Bill Webber of the "Curriculum for the Seventies" of the Association of Theological Schools. This document was developed by a group of eight seminary faculty from across the nation, Webber being one of its members. As Webber states, "I was much influenced by 'the' project . . . for me, this 'Curriculum for the Seventies' became a fascinating model of what a seminary might be."

In the opinion of Webber, "New York Theological Seminary, its students and faculty, did not seem to have been very much caught up in the ferment of the sixties." Nevertheless, the social situation in 1968 (beginning of Webber's incumbency at NYTS) was a significant social framework impacting the seminary. Indeed it was a period marked by the hopes and frustrations of the four factors noted by Webber: the civil rights movement, war on poverty, the undeclared war in Vietnam, and the emerging feminist movement.

The informing sources of Webber's pilgrimage, along with the emerging ethos set by the social milieu of the late sixties, coupled with the opportunity of "reorienting" and "expanding" (not to say, performing "radical surgery" on) a dying institution—New York Theological Seminary—provided the matrix for a contextual theological model.

Overcoming institutional roadblocks at every turn—from perceptions of a liberal CEO in a "biblical" seminary, known for its inductive method of Bible study, to serious financial constraints and an ambivalent faculty, trustees, and alumni—marked the early stages of Webber's leadership. These roadblocks were not only overcome, but they became the foundational "pieces" in the transfiguration of a seminary. The successful story of NYTS and the many who contribute to it is duly acknowledged by Webber. What finally emerged is noteworthy. A committed board and administration, a dedicated and much-gifted faculty and staff, and many friends and supporters, including a highly motivated and hardworking student body, share a special part in the success of this theological educational experiment.

The contextual theological educational model put in place by Webber centered in bridging the perennial dichotomy between "theory and practice," prevalent in most theological seminaries. This contextual model is informed by the need to teach effectiveness in that kind of ministerial training that endeavors to be faithful to its mission in an urbanized society.

Primacy of its Constituency Focus. The make-up of the constituency of NYTS under Webber's leadership shifted dramatically. What might appear as changes predicated on financial and student enrollment deficits, or worse on expediency or opportunism, should be viewed within the framework of Webber's integrity, vision, and, ultimately and most critically, his openness to the "leading of the Spirit." The "leading of the Spirit" is quite obvious in the seminary's willingness to focus its resources on its constituency. It seems, perhaps, trite to say this in view that all seminaries claim the same, yet by noting NYTS's teaching sites at Maine, Washington, D.C., Sheffield, England, and even Sing-Sing prison, one underscores its constituency focus. Even more impressive to me, as a Puerto Rican, is the response of NYTS to the Hispanic and African American church leadership—both clergy and laity—in New York City.

Traditional seminaries have implicitly said to Hispanics and African American church leadership (to underline but the two most dominant ethnic minorities in New York City), if you want a fully accredited (ATS) theological training, you must "jump the hoop" of a university degree, study in "our" campus, and study "our" theology (from "our" cultural and ideological perspective, of course). Come to us and we will send you back to your community of ministry with the "best" in theological education. This imperialistic attitude by traditional seminaries has meant either complete neglect of a significant constituency that makes up our major cities, or by and large, an irrelevant and decontextualized training for ministry and ethnic leadership.

New York Theological Seminary has become a model for many, of not only contextual theological education, but its corollary of a "globalized" constituency—reflecting the global nature of modern urban society. The African American, Hispanic, and most recently Korean program elements are a proof of this. Classes are taught in three languages—English, Spanish, and Korean. This constituency comes from not just your mainline denominations and churches, but from the pentecostal, holiness, and storefront communities of faith which literally dot the "barrios" and the "ghettos" of New York City.

Programmatic Development. The program pattern that developed at New York Theological Seminary responds to the varied constituency make-up of the city. Its theological training needs are reflected in a curriculum that accepts the church leader as he/she is. The college program has filled a critical need in the minority constituency. The certificate program has permitted serious theological training for those experienced ministers and church leaders that previously have been denied such training. These two programs have proved to be an excellent feeder to the seminary degree program level; thus facilitating a natural and reachable development of educational goals for its constituency.

The programmatic development at NYTS has been an opportunity to model empowerment, and shalom in theological education. Dr. Robert W. Pazmino states it well, "By empowering minorities on such an extensive scale, the programs at New York Theological Seminary have sought to address the problems of imposition and domination in the theological education of minority groups. Such imposition and domination were the common experience of minorities in traditional academic models that have not affirmed the place of alternative perspective."

Concluding Remarks. New York Theological Seminary as a "unique" theological institution, as a "pilgrim seminary," represents a sound model with its emphasis on the Bible in the training for ministry. Since World War II theological education has been experiencing a shift from "clerical" to the "people of God" paradigm. The degree to which New York Theological Seminary is able to serve the whole "people of God"—be they clergy or laity—will, in my opinion, depend on the new leadership keeping before its eyes the "pilgrim seminary" model that emerged under Bill Webber. This "pilgrim seminary" model speaks of a contextual theological education philosophy that responds to a "global" constituency with relevant and creative programs. Ultimately, a "pilgrim seminary" invests in people not in bricks, serves the whole body of Christ and not just an elite white, male, middle class, mainline denomination constituency; it knows that it is a sojourner viable only as a faithful missionary arm of the church of our Lord Jesus Christ.

Sr. Dorothy Ann Kelly, OSU
President, College of New Rochelle,
New Rochelle, N.Y.

Why are some institutions, indeed, why are some people, able to respond to periods of crisis with creative energy? The story recorded here of New York Theological Seminary's journey illustrates the combination of grace and ingenuity that enabled NYTS to change so radically in response to the leading of the Spirit. As one who is involved in one phase of this story (the partnership between the seminary and the College of New Rochelle), I am happy to see this history because of its inspirational value for those engaged in the work of the church and in the work of higher education.

In describing the actions of NYTS that resulted in the dismantling of its traditional educational program, Bill Webber lays claim to neither a "great new vision nor any special wisdom in the process but rather a desperate crisis which had forced the seminary to discover a new sense of its vocation."

The legacy of a nine-year struggle for funds and students brought the institution to a moment of truth in 1969 that was both desperate and freeing. It enabled Bill Webber and his colleagues to embark on a decade of experimentation. The saving grace in their flexibility and willingness to try different approaches to theological education was, I believe, their grounding in the mission of NYTS to serve the professional needs of the ministers of the church in New York City. If it was a different city, with a new preponderance of black and Hispanic churches, then a seminary seeking to educate the new ministers had to know and address their needs. The dialogue between the leaders of the seminary and the new urban ministers revealed the inadequacy of traditional programs and the failure of efforts to fit the new ministers into the old programs. These ministers, who were the natural leaders of their religious congregations in all their peoples' struggles with the city, had no access to a seminary or college education. NYTS's willingness to work creatively in this new situation brought the seminary and the College of New Rochelle into a close alliance beginning in 1977.

When Bill Webber first contacted me with the request to

bring our college program for adults (School of New Resources College of New Rochelle) to the seminary, I was going through an experience at CNR very similar to that which Bill was encountering at the seminary. In 1970 the College of New Rochelle faced the acute need to broaden its programs and appeal to new student markets. We examined the mission of the college which, since 1904, had been to make a college education available to those undeserved by other institutions, beginning with young women from Catholic family backgrounds. By the 1970s the aspirations of adults for a college program adapted to their situations appealed to our sense of the mission of the college in the last decades of the century. To this end, we developed a special liberal arts curriculum and a teaching staff which took the conditions and hopes of the adult student seriously. Response to the New Resources Program was so gratifying that we had difficulty keeping up with the requests for extensions of the program into various parts of New York City. In 1972 we opened the Program in New Rochelle and at DC-37 headquarters (American Federation of State, County, and Municipal Employees) in lower New York City. A year later, in response to requests, we started a branch campus in Co-op City and in the next two years one in the South Bronx, followed by the request from Bill Webber.

The College of New Rochelle had learned to listen to the needs of adult students, especially blacks and Hispanics, in New York City and to design a program of respect, support, and learning for them. Bill knew the church leaders who wanted to work for an undergraduate degree needed access to federal and state funding for their college education, the stimulation of classes designed for them, and a faculty who understood and respected their goals. New Resources was a great match for the seminary's needs. I am proud of the partnership between the seminary and the college which is part of the NYTS story.

The past fifteen-year period has been traumatic for seminary and college education. The time has come for reflections like this one on NYTS that can help us assess what has happened and even learn some lessons for the future. This is not just another story but a unique tribute to a pilgrim seminary where openness to the Spirit illuminated the way to remain true to an institutional mission in its deepest reality.

Robert Wood Lynn
Senior Vice President, Religion (Ret.)
Lilly Endowment, Inc.

One of the best recent books about American religion is Sidney E. Mead's *The Lively Experiment*. The full title of this brilliant work nicely catches the author's intent: The spirit of a "lively experiment" pervades the "shaping of Christianity in America."

That same spirit shows up intermittently in the history of American theological education. It becomes evident, for instance, in the early years of Andover, our country's first formative theological seminary. In the intervening decades other institutions have become powerful—though often momentary—lively experiments.

Only a handful of schools has embodied that spirit during the last twenty years. In this book, G. William (Bill) Webber tells the beguiling story of one of those exceptional institutions. Close to extinction in the late 1960s, New York Theological Seminary has enjoyed an astonishing renewal over the 1970s and 1980s. This "death and resurrection" story deserves to be studied carefully by theological educators in North America. For here is a reminder of how a school can come to life if several elements are present.

The first precondition is the presence of a resilient and imaginative faculty leader. Bill Webber certainly met that requirement. All that he had done in his earlier ministry prepared him for the extraordinary challenge of leading New York Theological Seminary toward reformation. His years at Union Theological Seminary (New York City) as a dean and professor opened up ways of understanding the larger enterprise of American theological education. One of the founders of the East Harlem Protestant Parish, Bill was consistently attentive to the major reformist efforts in urban ministry during the 1950s and 1960s. Most importantly, his own deep faith and willingness to take chances liberated him from the anxieties and timidities that hobbled so many middle class academics and church leaders. Few of us could have matched his inner calm in meeting the steady stream of crises at NYTS in the early 1970s.

Yet even the extraordinary talents of a Bill Webber would have proved inadequate in these crises if there had not been crucial support forthcoming from two other quarters—the faculty and the trustees. Someday, perhaps the faculty who served the seminary both "before" and "after" the upheavals of the late 1960s could tell us more about how it felt to be part of an institution whose future appeared so uncertain. In the meantime, however, I am intrigued by the way most faculty members helped. Sometimes they aided the cause by resigning (without holding the institution hostage to lawsuits). Or sometimes they contributed notably by accepting new and demanding teaching assignments. Their example could well inspire other seminary faculties whose institutions may be next on the critical list of "endangered" North American theological schools.

Likewise, trustees in other seminaries could benefit from reading this absorbing account. Unlike most authors of "in-house" histories of theological schools, Bill Webber included the trustees in his narrative. Consequently, the reader gains a rare glimpse of a board acting in the midst of various crises. In retrospect, the trustees' participation proved crucial and creative at a number of junctures. Moreover, the board underwent a dramatic transformation in less than a decade. The complete story of that revolution in such a short span of time could offer American seminaries an apt "case study" of responsible trusteeship.

By means of a mysterious alchemy, these three elements worked together to help the seminary face openly and courageously the awesome question which finally any institution must answer in one way or another—"Whom do we serve and for what purpose?" During the 1970s, New York Theological Seminary discovered its new publics and its enlivening purpose. Or, perhaps more to the point, certain churches and ethnic groups found this institution and made it into a genuinely contemporary New York theological school. Therein lies the heart of this appealing story. Without that powerful sense of mutual discovery, NYTS would not be the institution it is today.

Why cannot other institutions tell the same story? That is a question which I have asked myself ever since the late 1970s when I first became aware of this exciting tale. For the last ten years, I have hoped that other theological schools located in the great urban areas of America might learn from this venture of faith. Here, at last, is the text which might prompt those theological educators to ponder the question—"Whom do we serve and for what purpose?"

Gayraud Wilmore
Professor (Church History),
Interdenominational Theological Seminary,
Atlanta, Georgia

I want to thank Bill Webber for taking the time and effort to give us this remarkable review of the evolution of one of the first truly urban, ethnically pluralistic, biblically centered, while socially and politically radical, educational institutions for the equipment of both clerical and lay leadership for the church of the twenty-first century.

The story certainly needed to be told as an example of the gracious action of God upon the "secular city." Bill has given, at the same time, due emphasis upon the faith, hope, and love of many persons who worked together over the years to make NYTS possible in the closing years of the twentieth century.

I suspect that many would agree that the most exciting and significant thing about the story is the shift. From a basically traditional theological education program for middle-class white men and a few white women, well into the 1960s, NYTS became a program for primarily black and Hispanic men and women. Most of these students were poor, some burdened with personal problems related to marginality, and almost all of them limited in their preparedness for serious graduate studies. Yet they were eager to become competent leaders in their respective communities.

No other "white-led" graduate institution in the field of religion has taken that task (education for ministry for minority persons) more seriously than NYTS. Although this book is a very good report of its commitment, I am not sure that the dramatic transition has been fully acknowledged and that sufficient implications have been drawn for NYTS trustees, administration, and faculty. The revolution is yet incomplete in that regard and something should be said not only about the sincere effort being made to complete it, but also about the ambiguities, frustrations, and difficulties encountered along the way. White women, for example, have found a solid place at all levels, and for that we are thankful. But the same cannot yet be said for black and Hispanic men and women. This fact should not be treated casually or ignored.

But many good and instructive lessons come through this history: the *koinonia* of the seminary family, the place of prayer, Bible study and community-building experiences, the face turned deliberately toward the streets of New York (although much of that is still more intention than fact), the innovative, experimental spirit of the place, the celebration of urbanity and secularity, the concern for previously neglected and submerged minorities now presenting their claim for a place in the ecumenical church.

These emphases should not only be retained now that NYTS has once again joined the list of fully accredited theological seminaries, but it should be urgently commended to other predominantly white and predominantly black institutions whose contexts have not offered the same opportunities for radical transformation that NYTS experienced.

This excellent monograph by the uncontested dean of nontraditional, urban, cross-cultural theological education, Bill Webber, goes a long way toward making this wider application possible.

APPENDIX A

To: Board of Directors, NYTS
From: George W. Webber
Date: February 3, 1969

RE: The Future of the New York Theological Seminary

I. Introduction

During the month of January, I have spent a great deal of time seeking to understand the history and traditions of the New York Theological Seminary in order to gain a perspective from which to consider the appropriateness of my assumption of the presidency. From this study of the past has emerged a fairly clear picture of the present situation of the seminary with its sobering problems and ambiguous future. I personally hope that these present difficulties can be surmounted and the seminary fulfill its potential as a vital and creative instrument in theological education. This memorandum is an attempt to set forth my vision of what the future might involve in order that board and faculty alike may have a further basis for determining whether in fact I should be called to the presidency of the seminary. Only as we share a common vision might we hope to bring about the miracle of renewal.

II. Reflections on History

In my process of study and evaluation I have been relieved to discover the vitality and viability of the traditions of the seminary. I can affirm with enthusiasm the purposes of the seminary as set forth in the bylaws. To me, the essential nature of Christianity as a biblical faith is beyond question. The heritage of an institution committed to continual seriousness before the demand of solid Bible study is altogether congenial. Further, the insistence of the founders that freedom of interpretation must be given to the individual seems to be a glorious guarantee that the seminary never fall into the possession of any theological camp. It may be the case that some among the alumni and friends, of one theological persuasion or another, may feel that only their position is faithful to Biblical Seminary. I can find no support for this assumption in my reading of the history. At the same time, I would personally do all in my power to alienate no element of the alumni by seeking to denigrate any theological position in contrast to my own.

In addition to a vital heritage of biblical learning, the seminary has also been a notably pioneering institution, using its small size and flexibility to experiment with much greater freedom than many well known seminaries. Dr. White was apparently not interested in founding just another seminary, but was determined that this institution must always fulfill a unique, prophetic, pioneering role in theological education.

Dr. White was also aware of the importance of the location of the seminary in the heart of New York City. Clearly part of the uniqueness of the seminary would lie in exploiting its location in training men and women for ministry.

I believe that in building a future, the seminary must affirm these three elements in its heritage: solid biblical learning, a pioneering role in theological education, and its urban location. Perhaps a rational evaluation of the present state of the seminary would lead to the conclusion that immediate steps should be taken to close the institution. I believe that the churches in our time are being significantly short-changed by theological seminaries. There is almost desperate and certainly urgent need for radical experimentation in equipping men and women for ministry and mission in the emerging world. Perhaps alone in this country the New York Theological Seminary, with its unique history and location, might venture the risks of such experimentation. I am convinced that the only other option is to close.

III. A Program for the Seminary

In the course of recent weeks, I have discussed with the board, faculty, and students some of my concerns about theological education. By the end of the weekend long-range planning conference, the main outlines of what I would now suggest as the program for the immediate future of the seminary had taken shape. Here, in quite summary form are the main elements:

A. Basic programs for BD and MRE students
   1. Radical educational experiment for full-time BD and MRE students: two-year program, appropriate for this faculty, from the AATS "Curriculum for the Seventies"; to be followed by one year of directed work in ministry; admit forty students in September 1969;
   2. Service to all seminaries directly
      a. Metropolitan Intern Year, now run by MUST.
      b. Urban term for seminaries—either a semester or a year for students from any seminary that would like us to specialize in urban orientation and training;
   3. Implementation: all three elements could be undertaken by the fall. This will demand intense work on the part of faculty over the next five months.

B. Continuing Education
   1. Degree Programs
      This involves the continuation of the present basic programs in STM work:
      a. Counseling
      b. Urban Ministries
      and adding
      c. International Affairs.

2. Nondegree programs
    a. Programs developed with storefront and Pentecostal pastors;
    b. Programs for Roman Catholic nuns (may also fall under degree programs).

C. And in the near future, I suggest two additional emphases:
1. Lay theological training in mission and ministry;
2. Theological "Think Tank" for the churches in this metropolitan area.

A host of problems must be resolved in putting such a program into immediate operation. But I am persuaded that we have the resources to move ahead at once. In part this confidence arises because the presence of MUST provides resources that are essential in developing an effective role as a center for training in mission in an urban world. Some of the matters to be faced at once are:

1. Recruitment of entering BD students;
2. Adequate care for present students, including their participation in planning;
3. Explanation of our programs available to other seminaries;
4. Clarity about what the experimental curriculum will demand of faculty and students.

IV. Essential Elements for Proceeding

I hope it is obvious by now that I am tremendously enthusiastic about the pioneering role the seminary might play in the years ahead. But my enthusiasm must be matched by an equal commitment on the part of the board of directors and the faculty. Therefore, I request the faculty to convey to the board fully and with candor their position in regard to my possible selection as president and their degree of commitment to a program along the general lines of this memo. We must not proceed forward together until there is enthusiastic common agreement on our goals for the seminary. By the same token, I request the board to give careful consideration to this memo before taking any legal vote on my name.

Let me be quite candid in terms of my assessment of both these crucial elements in the future of the seminary. The faculty is remarkably competent and provides, as far as I am now able to judge, an adequate basis for theological education along the lines I am suggesting.

The board of directors, however, is another story. The small number of able and committed members does not seem to provide the strength needed for the future. Nor do there seem to be many members who have either brought to bear insight into the task of the seminary or assisted significantly in raising funds. I would thus feel it essential at once to bring the board to full strength and to follow the mandate of the bylaws in dropping those who have failed to meet the requirements of attendance. In an appendix I have listed my suggestions for new board members and would propose that I be authorized to approach them at once for permission to propose them for election.

Finally, the most sobering element in the present decision-making process is the matter of finances. Clearly, the president must play a key role in funding the programs of the institution, but by the same token, he must provide at this point in history significant leadership in educational policy and implementation. It would be wonderful if there were funds in hand for eighteen months while we undertake an educational evolution of some magnitude. But the harsh facts seem to indicate that there is simply no fat left in the assets of the seminary. I am at a loss to discover how it is anticipated to meet the deficit for the present academic year or what sources of funds might possibly make it logical for the board to enter into another academic year. Some understanding of board thinking on this matter would be helpful to me. To put the matter bluntly, with no large expansion in the seminary budget, how much money does the new president have to raise to keep afloat until May 31, 1970? What leads the board to believe that such an amount could in fact be raised?

V. Consummation of the Relationship?

It is clear that time is running out in terms of a decision about the presidency. I devoutly hope that the board will have the legal ability on February 20, 1969, to take the definite action, if that is appropriate. At the moment, the board has not extended a legal call and has every right to give full and careful consideration to this before voting. Unless the elements in this letter are acceptable, or have been negotiated with me further, I would not think it appropriate for me to accept a proffered call. The advise and consent of the faculty is a key element also and I hope this can be made available to the board by February 20. I am also sending a copy of this memo to the president of the student council, with the thought that the student officers may also wish to communicate with the board.

Assuming the decision of the board and faculty to extend the call, the only serious remaining problem from my side is the need for further clarity about the financial issues that face the seminary. I shall seek further insight during the next two weeks, but suspect that this matter will need attention on February 20.

From the point of view of the board, my present commitments may present severe, even insuperable problems. During the next three months I am committed to an extremely heavy academic load that cannot at this date be altered. By serious curtailment of MUST staff assignments and recreation, I could break free two full days a week to devote to: a) fund raising, b) educational policy development with the faculty and students, and c) initial interpretation of our program to seminaries and colleges. Full-time duties could thus begin only June 1, 1969. In the second place I have agreed to spend a block of time in the spring of 1970 as a visiting professor at John Carroll University. This will require me to be away from 1:00 p.m. on Monday through Tuesday for fifteen weeks.

VI. Conclusion

I have sought to be entirely candid in this memo. I hope that board, faculty and students will reply in kind. Only a relationship of trust and confidence will give us any hope in finding our way into a creative future together. I am eager to enter into further discussion at any point. I also affirm the right of board and/or faculty to withdraw from further negotiations without prejudice.

cc: Student Council officers.

APPENDIX B

Key Administrative Faculty Persons and Staff 1969–1983

William Weisenbach (1969–) Presbyterian

He graduated from the seminary in 1969 and accepted a position as assistant to the president. He willingly undertook every assignment I could give him—personnel to maintenance, dealing with alumni and producing the *Bulletin*, providing moral support and pinch hitting (finances and curriculum planning . . . just about any imaginable task). His own competence and wisdom led to his election as vice-president in 1974. He was instrumental in the development of every major program undertaken since 1971. Many of our most significant decisions were the result of his suggestion, common sense, or imagination. He was an invaluable colleague and friend over all the years of my presidency.

Melvin Schoonover (1969–1977) American Baptist

We had been colleagues in East Harlem following his graduation from Union Theological Seminary in 1956. He was called to the seminary my first year to oversee the work on continuing education for clergy in urban ministry. That led to his appointment to the faculty eventually with responsibility for both the STM degree and the development and implementation of our DMin. He was an excellent teacher and a fine administrator.

Willis Elliott (1969–1979) United Church of Christ

His initial assignment was to develop our lay education programs. But his remarkable gifts as scholar and teacher resulted in his teaching a heavy load in biblical theology and ethics. The Second Career program (also called Mid-Career Exploration) was a very creative response to the cry of lay persons for an opportunity to do serious theological study in a convenient time slot.

John Kildahl (1969–1974) American Lutheran Church

An ordained clergyman and psychotherapist in private practice, he initiated the STM program in pastoral care during the presidency of Bonnell. An excellent teacher and wise counselor to the new president, he continued to teach through 1983.

Thomas Boomershine (1972–1979) United Methodist

As a result of the study by the alumni of the new era at NYTS, the trustees voted to establish the Wilbert Webster White chair in Biblical Studies. Tom Boomershine was a superb choice. Just completing his PhD at Union, he brought a commitment to biblical storytelling that was thoroughly compatible with the traditional method of inductive Bible study. His presence helped assure that all our work expressed a solid biblical commitment.

Eadras Betancourt (1973–1976) Assembly of Christian Churches

A graduate of New York Theological Seminary in 1971, he was called as first administrator of the college program developed with Adelphi University. Standing firmly in the Hispanic Pentecostal tradition, he provided a vital bridge to the strong Hispanic Protestant community. He also laid the groundwork for our joint MDiv program through developing an Urban Year for Hispanic students.

Robert Washington (1973–1983) Presbyterian

A leading layman in the united Presbyterian Church, he joined the faculty as dean of black studies. Deeply trusted by our students, black, Hispanic, and white, he was responsible for developing our first Saturday Certificate Program at NYTS. His status as a lay person enabled him to relate effectively to a wide range of black churches.

DIANA BEACH (1975–1983) EPISCOPAL

Originally hired to assist Mel Schoonover with degree programs, she quickly established herself as an excellent teacher in the field of pastoral theology. Her input as a feminist also made an important contribution. We rejoiced in her ordination several years after joining the administrative faculty.

JOSE CARABALLO (1976–) PRESBYTERIAN (INITIALLY ASSEMBLIES OF GOD)

The first graduate of our college program, he succeeded Betancourt as dean of Hispanic studies. He is an outstanding leader in the Hispanic religious community, both Pentecostal and mainline. His credibility made possible the development of the Certificate Program in Spanish. A man of deep and convicting faith, he has been affirmed as the most sensitive offerer of public prayer among the faculty.

KATIE CANNON (1977–1980) PRESBYTERIAN

She was called to assist in the English Certificate Program. She did an excellent job in undergirding its development. She was also a fine teacher in ethics in the degree programs as well as in certificate courses. She left to complete her doctorate.

KEITH RUSSELL (1978–) AMERICAN BAPTIST

He was persuaded to leave a parish in Albany, New York, to take on a dual assignment in NYC: member of the administrative faculty and pastor of an inner-city church in Brooklyn, each on a half-time basis. His primary assignment was to teach in both the DMin and STM in Parish Ministry programs. Trusted by all, theologically insightful, he is a man of compassion and faith.

T. RICHARD SNYDER (1978–) PRESBYTERIAN

For some years prior to joining the administrative faculty, Dick Snyder was a very creative adjunct teacher, developing the first STM program in Maine, and then serving as the director of ISTEM. He took over many of the responsibilities of Mel Schoonover, beginning in 1978. An excellent teacher, he took administrative oversight of both the STM and DMin programs.

Norman Gottwald (1980–) American Baptist

He was willing to leave a tenured position on the Graduate Theological Faculty in Berkeley to join NYTS. He succeeded Tom Boomershine in the biblical studies chair. He has been willing to make the adjustments required for a traditional scholar to share the load at NYTS. His open and nondefensive manner as a teacher makes it possible for him to work effectively with our diverse student body.

Emily Gibbes (1981–) Presbyterian

Born and educated in New York City, Emily Gibbes has been a trustee of the seminary. After her retirement from a long and distinguished career in Christian education, she accepted a position on the faculty to develop our degree work in Christian education. Her contribution as teacher, as a black woman, and as a colleague has been immense.

Samuel Solivan (1982–) Reformed Church in America

Although raised in a Pentecostal church in East Harlem, he had served as a Reformed Church missionary in South America. An effective teacher in theology, he made a significant contribution in the first year of the prison program as well as in the Hispanic certificate courses.

The following is a partial list of crucial members of the support staff:

Patti Eastep, secretary to the president for six years–highly skilled, excellent peripheral vision, and committed to our task.

Ilene Grandison, a compassionate and sensitive assistant in developing the Saturday certificate program.

Paul Jensen, comptroller for the years of the transition–competent and committed to the seminary.

Svea Murphy, long-time bookkeeper–meticulous and hardworking, and with a good disposition, in spite of all.

Margaret Rathum, here long before 1969, registrar, source of all information about students, secretary to Mel Schoonover–always reliable.

Desmond Roberts, loyal and hardworking man for all tasks–mail room, switchboard, and anything else needed to keep us operating.

Maria Rosa, secretary to the Hispanic programs–efficient and caring, sometimes the only Spanish speaker on hand.

Eleanor Soler, became the librarian in the early years; betook herself to library school and developed a high level of professional competence–always helpful to students and faculty alike.

APPENDIX C

Reflections on the Overall Task
July 1979

As we discussed at our first meeting, NYTS has a unique opportunity to undertake creative educational ministries without many of the traditional restraints of most theological seminaries. We thus have a strong obligation to use our freedom and flexibility to the best ends possible. Having operated for ten years without much careful planning or with any significant attention to our administrative patterns, it now seems useful to get a fix on our present position and give thought to our goals, style, and funding for the years ahead.

The Planning Committee is thus assuming the task of creating a long-range planning operation, our plans for the future, and a program for their implementation. The components of such a planning document will include at least these:

1. Evaluation of our present educational programs—leading to the details of a functioning program of ongoing evaluation for all elements of the seminary and for continuing planning;
2. Clear understanding of what we seek in terms of the role of trustees and how we can achieve such a membership;

3. Agreement on the basic goals and purposes of the seminary with strategy for achieving them;
4. A carefully defined and initially implemented development program;
5. Development of an efficient and appropriate administrative structure and support services;
6. A job description and profile for the next president, and a program for selection and transition.

What follows are suggestions on how to go about dealing with each of these components.

I. The Basic Elements of our Task: Evaluation of our present education program and plans for the future work in evaluation and planning.

   A. The Task: A critical overview of our present education programs. This requires us to implement effectively our present commitments to evaluation of programs (for example, better than we have been doing) and then seek outside evaluation both of our methods and of the results.

      Wheeler suggests, we need a thoughtful overview by an outsider who knows the field of alternative theological education, is sympathetic to it, and who can make a critical achievement of the NYTS programs. It will be important to seek advice and evaluation from those who are graduates of each of our programs in addition to the work Mel Schoonover has been doing with our STM graduates.

   B. Examine our present systems of evaluation for programs and personnel. Make recommendations for improvement and implementation and work on how we can continue to build into our ongoing life a program of planning and development in program areas.

   C. Research methods: implementation of present commitments. Employment of a consultant to evaluate our work and the data (perhaps two different persons).

D. Task Force:
   1. Trustees: Fields, Gibbes, Schoonover, Quiroga
   2. Staff: Webber, Weidenbach
   3. Research: Several from outside with some ad hoc advisers also.

II. The Appropriate Role and Functioning of the Trustees.
   A. The Task: Assess the effectiveness of the board as presently constituted—the make-up and selection process, the roles board members play, the usefulness of the program committees, relation to the administration, role in decision making;
   B. Develop a model for an appropriate board for this institution in as much detail as possible and in dialogue with the present board, administration, and faculty, and those outside with experience;
   C. Additional Comments: May wish to look at the "servant" booklets of Robert Greenleaf as a starting point. This area should also be one for major attention by the NESC personnel.
   D. Task Force:
      1. Trustees: Newbold, Davidson, Baron, Van Dusen
      2. Staff: Webber
      3. Consultant: NESC personnel, with consultancy session with others as needed.

III. Purpose and Goals of the Seminary: A Look at the Future
   A. The Task: Examine our present statements of self-understanding and purpose, revising them as necessary. On the basis of this, do research on the emerging needs that may fall in our purview in the next ten years and make recommendations for policy decisions where appropriate. This relates quite directly to Project II in the Wheeler document. Her statement should be considered as part of this section.
   B. Research Method: Will need to find a person who can review present research, consult with church executives and others concerned about educational needs for clergy and laity, and conduct informal sur-

T

U

V

W

X

Y

Z

Carlo Suarès (1892–1976) dedicated a great part of his life to unraveling symbolism hidden in the code of the Bible. Born in Egypt, he studied in Paris and has written many notable books, including *The Cipher of Genesis*, also published by Weiser.

veys of our present and recent student population. One suspects that a range of clues, hunches, fantasies, etc., might emerge that would then be sifted, evaluated, given shape by the Planning Committee. These would be compared with our present programs in the process of proposing changed or new directions. The two fundamental questions are these:

1. What are the trends, directions, etc., we need to take into account for the development of seminary programs?
2. How do we institutionalize this process of keeping open the future?

C. Task Force:

1. Trustees: Eddy, Stanton, Larasraud, and Zwernemann
2. Staff: Russell, Caraballo, Washington and Beach
3. Researcher: From outside; to be selected.

IV. Design for a Development Program

A. The Task: The examination of all our present efforts in the whole area of development including fund-raising, public relations, etc. The design and implementation of a comprehensive program of development with appropriate schedules, goals for the future, and the implications for administration, trustees, and the institution as a whole. The task should also do as much of Project III in the Wheeler report as considered useful.

B. Research Method: Midtbo, with Webber, to provide data on the recent history of fund-raising and public relations. Then new development personnel and NESC volunteer work on design for the future.

C. Task Force:

1. Trustees: Barry, with Irish, Sherard, Erazo, Caliandro
2. Staff: Hopley, with Midtbo, Webber, Daniel
3. Consultants: NESC personnel; outside as necessary for image assessment.

V. Administration, Governance, and Support Systems

A. The Task: Assess the present operation in these areas, with attention to adequacy of staffing arrangements, the efforts of combined teaching and administrative functions, the level of staff and administrative support salaries, other personnel policies, the role and effectiveness of business operations and use of space—all for the sake of recommendations for improvement or change.

B. Research Method: Action/research, with aid of our outside personnel who will conduct interviews and examine our present scene (cf. Wheeler, Section I).

VI. Profile, Job Description, and Transition Process for Next President: This is the basic task of the planning committee and the trustees. Suggest that the full committee see this as its assignment. Need to spell out more fully the details of this section of our work.

Led By the Spirit
Webber George 44
0829808507 07/12/94 JJJ
Fall94 M-Div <1270>
37135 Pilgri
07/12/94 Pilgri $11.95